T3-AKC-131

# Managing Public Finances in a Small Developing Economy

# Managing Public Finances in a Small Developing Economy

## The Case of Barbados

### Marion V. Williams

**Westport, Connecticut**
**London**

336.729
W 72m

**Library of Congress Cataloging-in-Publication Data**

Williams, Marion V.
    Managing public finances in a small developing economy : the case of Barbados /
Marion V. Williams.
        p.   cm.
    ISBN 0–275–97031–0 (alk. paper)
    1. Finance, Public—Barbados.  I. Title.
HJ867.W55    2001
336.72981—dc21          00–042750

British Library Cataloguing in Publication Data is available.

Copyright © 2001 by Marion V. Williams

All rights reserved. No portion of this book may be
reproduced, by any process or technique, without the
express written consent of the publisher.

Library of Congress Catalog Card Number: 00–042750
ISBN: 0–275–97031–0

First published in 2001

Praeger Publishers, 88 Post Road West, Westport, CT 06881
An imprint of Greenwood Publishing Group, Inc.
www.praeger.com

Printed in the United States of America

The paper used in this book complies with the
Permanent Paper Standard issued by the National
Information Standards Organization (Z39.48–1984).

10  9  8  7  6  5  4  3  2  1

For my late mother, Cledlene

University Libraries
Carnegie Mellon University
Pittsburgh PA 15213-3890

# Contents

# Illustrations

**FIGURES**

# Symbols and Abbreviations

| | |
|---|---|
| .. | Not applicable or not available |
| – | None or Negligible |
| B'dos | Barbados |
| BDS$ | Barbados Dollar |
| BIDC | Barbados Investment Development Corporation |
| BIMAP | Barbados Institute of Management and Productivity |
| BIS | Bank for International Settlements |
| BOT | Build, Operate and Transfer |
| CARICOM | Caribbean Community and Common Market |
| CDW | Colonial Development and Welfare |
| CET | Common External Tariff |
| CFATF | Caribbean Financial Action Task Force |
| CIDA | Canadian International Development Agency |
| CIF | Cost, Insurance and Freight |
| CMCF | Caribbean Multilateral Clearing Facility |
| CPI | Consumer Price Index |
| DW | Durbin-Watson Statistic |
| E | Estimate |
| EP | Effective Protection |
| FATF | Financial Action Task Force |
| FSF | Financial Stability Forum |
| GATS | General Agreement on Trade in Services |
| GATT | General Agreement on Trade and Tariffs |
| GDP | Gross Domestic Product |
| GNP | Gross National Product |

| HIPC | Highly Indebted Poor Countries |
|------|-------------------------------|
| IADB | Inter-American Development Bank |
| IBCs | International Business Companies |
| IBRD | International Bank for Reconstruction and Development |
| IFI | International Financial Institutions |
| IMF | International Monetary Fund |
| Inf | Inflation |
| J'ca | Jamaica |
| J$ | Jamaica Dollars |
| MFN | Most Favored Nation |
| MC | Marginal Cost |
| MS | Money Supply |
| OECD | Organization for Economic Cooperation and Development |
| p | Provisional |
| PAYE | Pay as You Earn |
| R and D | Research and Development |
| RR | Reserve Requirements as a Percentage of Total Assets |
| S.E. | Standard Error |
| SD | Standard Deviation |
| Ser. cor. | Serial Correlation |
| SRLs | Societies with Restricted Liability |
| $SSE_r$ | Restricted Sum of Squares |
| $SSE_u$ | Unrestricted Sum of Squares |
| TB | Treasury Bill yield |
| T'dad & T'go or T & T | Trinidad and Tobago |
| TEA | Tax Information Exchange Agreement |
| TT$ | Trinidad and Tobago dollars |
| UK | United Kingdom |
| UNDP | United Nations Development Program |
| SAID | United States Agency for International Development |
| VAT | Value added tax |
| WTO | World Trade Organization |

# Preface

The study of public finance encompasses one of the remaining areas of political economy from which it has proved difficult to disengage economic laws and principles from moral and value judgments about national economic goals. Nineteenth century economists tried to formulate general laws and principles of economic behavior uncomplicated by reference to historical and sociological decisions. However, the record shows that in the study of public finance this is not always possible. Most models of economic development include some social variables, and many models of economic behavior are based on some view of human reaction that guides economic behavior.

Historically, governments were seen as performing a countervailing role to the public sector, and distribution of incomes through public finances was an acceptable objective of governments, and they attempted in their management of public finances to introduce notions of economic efficiency. In the postwar period, the role of the state was expanding worldwide and there was an increasing tendency for central governments to extend their scope and to become involved in what were termed "market activities."

With the development of theories of public finance, governments increasingly saw themselves also as adopting budget strategies to control inflation, increase efficiency, redistribute incomes and promote economic growth. For small developing countries the constraints were much greater. Balance of payments equilibrium was a much more significant consideration as was improvement in the standard of living.

However, the priorities of some developing countries differ from those of developed economies, so that each country needs to be judged relative to its own objectives and not only by conventional standards of GNP. The UNDP Human Development Index is one way of introducing a level of measurement that differs from the conventional GNP per capita measure. Both measures are important, but the UNDP index introduces a measure of the quality of life that is favorable to countries that place the human condition high on their agendas. The consequential argument, however, is whether a country should aim first for a high rate of growth of per capita income and allow the quality of life to flow from that achievement or vice versa.

This book discusses how Barbados, a small developing country, fashioned an approach to public finance management that permitted it to become the leading developing country in the Human Development Index prepared by UNDP while achieving moderate rates of growth and maintaining macroeconomic stability.

# Acknowledgments

I would like to thank Professor Andrew Downes for his comments on the focus and structure of the book and for several other suggestions that were very helpful.

I also extend my thanks and deep appreciation to Muriel Saunders who provided me with statistical information relating to the 50-year period covered by the book. Thanks also to Dr. Roland Craigwell who offered useful comments.

I am also grateful to my secretary, Marcia Weekes, to Arlette King, and more especially, to Yvette Cheeseman, who helped with the typing and proofreading of the work.

My deepest thanks go to my family, especially my husband Clyde, who always gave me his unstinting support.

# 1

# Introduction

In articulating a role for the state as a manager of public finances at the beginning of the twenty-first century, it is instructive to first evaluate the role of the state as a public finance manager in the last century in order to learn lessons from that era.

A definition of the public sector as used in this book is first useful. The public sector is defined principally to include the central government and the local government[1] is included only insofar as their deficits were financed, and statutory boards only to the extent that they were a charge on the central budget.[2] The term "government" in this book will be used to mean the central government unless otherwise stated. However, some focus will be given to key statutory boards[3] and their contribution to public sector performance and more especially to the direct ownership role of government in industrial development.

At the beginning of the nineteenth century the notion still prevailed that the role of the state was to provide defense, protect property rights and enforce law and order. David Ricardo was the first to focus on the economy as a distinct entity from the state. He formulated general principles of economic behavior that distanced themselves from "historical, institutional, sociological, moral or philosophical dimensions" (Deane, 1989). By the early twentieth century his views and those of Adam Smith—which advocated that the society's good was maximized when each individual maximized his own gain—had begun to lose some force in the face of the economic reality of World War I, which saw a retreat into protectionism.

In the postwar period therefore, the redistribution of incomes through public finance became an accepted objective of government. Following

World War I, Keynes (1936) called for a more realistic perception of the need for government intervention in the modern economic system and for a loan-financed public works program for Britain. This changing role of the state saw central governments extending their scope into the "capitalist" markets.

Consequently, the three decades following the outbreak of World War II were labeled "the age of economic management" in Britain. In these years many developing colonial countries, many former colonies of Britain, gained their independence and adopted the Keynesian polices that had seen the United Kingdom through the postwar period.

Theories of economic development during this period assumed a major role for the state. By the 1950s government intervention in the economy was accepted and was aimed at correcting market failures, overcoming negative externalities, providing positive externalities and improving efficiency. Neo-Keynesian approaches to public finance and increased public ownership were accepted forms of public intervention up to the 1970s.

The 1980s however, witnessed a swing back to economic liberalization. International financial institutions joined forces to recommend a roll-back of state intervention and reductions in state ownership. Within the last two decades of the twentieth century therefore, it became fashionable to call for smaller government and for withdrawal of government from commercial activity. The persistently disappointing records of many third world countries, where government ownership and intervention had been the norm, fueled such calls. However, the disarray of many countries that had turned to developing market economies in the 1990s caused many to pause and reflect on the advocacy of smaller government in itself as an important prerequisite for good government, particularly in developing countries. Developed countries seemed less affected by this new paradigm. In fact, comparisons among countries at different levels of per capita income tended to show higher shares of government expenditures and of tax revenues in the higher income-earning countries than in lower income-earning countries.

At the same time it can be argued that some countries placed greater emphasis on economic development than on social development and that this was reflected in their governments' fiscal polices and in developmental priorities. However, for many years, until the creation of the UNDP Human Development Index, which compared countries on a cross-sectional basis using criteria of social development, there was no internationally recognized measure of their relative attainment in the area of social development. Budget outlays on these expenditures went unrecognized at the level of international comparisons of results as they related to standards of living.

The debate on the intervention of the state in the 1950s and 1960s was usually placed in the context of correction of market failure, not social achievements. The redistributional role of the state and its role in protecting certain groups in society was often given low emphasis in the literature on public finance.

However, if social costs and benefits are not effectively redistributed and are not fully reflected in market prices, then the outcome of the market could be suboptimal for society as a whole. The state may therefore need to intervene in particular markets in order to ensure that certain common goods are generally available. The financing of this imperative has implications for taxes and subsidies. Justification for such intervention is often placed in the context of the externalities from which investment projects can benefit as reflected in their ability to draw on a healthy and well-educated labor force.

Government intervention is sometimes also necessary in order to achieve an acceptable distribution of public goods. While direct production by government is one solution, other means of dealing with this type of market failure are possible. This often entails a careful prioritizing of expenditures, such as infrastructural expenditures relative to social expenditures. In small developing countries where problems of scale prevent rapid development of market driven initiatives, a greater responsibility tends to be placed on the state to perform the role of prioritizing these activities.

Normally, a high sustained rate of growth of real national income defines successful development (Lewis, 1984). However, the extent to which government intervenes to provide certain services often depends on whether the objective of government is to provide a better quality of life for its citizens or to achieve a higher rate of growth in GDP. Some countries are able to achieve a high level of development while achieving a moderate level of economic growth. Recent studies using the UNDP Human Development Index (UNDP Human Development Report, 1994) have sought to show how public finances contribute to human development. While other studies (Smith and Wahba, 1997) have demonstrated that the determinants of human development are different from the determinants of growth. They found that the growth of labor and spending on social activities are positively correlated with human development.

## PUBLIC FINANCE IN BARBADOS: AN OVERVIEW

Barbados finds itself in the upper layer of developing countries. In 1994 Barbados was the leading developing country in the Human Development Index published by the UNDP and continues to take a prominent position in these rankings. Though its rate of growth was not exceptionally high, compared to that of the Southeast Asian tigers, it was mostly positive, recording an average rate of real economic growth over the past half-century of about 2.2% per annum, well above that of many developing countries.

However, unlike many Latin American countries, the government sector never held a major share of economic activity, though it was important in many indirect ways in promoting such activity. Indeed, a detailed analysis of the role of the government sector in the economic development of Barbados shows it to be extremely important throughout the entire half-century of 1950–1999. During this time there were both obvious and imperceptible shifts in the approach of government to the management of the Barbadian economy. In the 1950s government performed mostly a caretaker role, maintaining order, providing basic services such as roads, postal services, water and defense, developing a legal framework and imposing taxes to finance these services. Significant shifts in the stance of government were evident in the 1960s when government began emphasizing industrial development, becoming directly involved as an equity holder in several major industrial enterprises, in tourism-related activities and in the provision of commercial services. In the 20 years that followed, this involvement accelerated, particularly following the achievement of independence. It was accompanied in the 1970s by a shift into direct equity involvement in the financial sector.[4] By the 1980s poor performance of many government-owned entities and lack-luster output of several statutory corporations led to a shift of philosophies, and prompted urgings by the private sector for government to voluntarily cease engagement in what were termed "commercial type" activities.

However, there was little effort by the domestic private sector to successfully fill the gap created by government's withdrawal. Indeed, except in the construction sector, the 1980s and 1990s saw very few major private sector activities of domestic origin of the size of government-owned projects of the 1970s.[5] Except for a few outstanding examples, major spurts in private sector ownership occurred only when government entities were privatized or otherwise sold into private ownership. There was however, significant activity at the level of the intermediate sized firm in the retail trade. In the late 1990s efforts were again made to achieve similar spurts in economic growth through incentives to private sector entities who were willing to assume responsibility for major developmental projects. However, most of these were real estate-related. By that time government seemed to have lost its appetite for industrial activity and concentrated its energies on social, developmental, and on facilitatory approaches to creating an environment in which a healthy private sector could thrive. Provision of adequate social and infrastructural services and concerns of macroeconomic stability tended to be the paramount preoccupations. Thus, the experience of the 1970s and 1980s suggests that markets may also fail to produce optimal outcomes. This aspect of private sector nonperformance can be described as a special case of market failure.

In differing ways therefore, the government sector was therefore undeniably of fundamental importance for the Barbadian economy during the last 50 years, both through direct involvement and indirect involvement as a facilitator and as a stabilizing agent. Its mode of operation contributed significantly to stable government and a stable economy.

In the first 25 years following the middle of the century, the desire for rapid economic and social development led the country to give an expanding role to government activities. By 1975 government controlled the flow of 16.1% of national product employed 26% of the labor force, but owned only a small proportion of productive assets. Budgets were aimed to formulate tax policies designed to stimulate economic growth, to ensure efficiency in the disbursement of funds, to control inflation and to improve the balance of payments.[6] The second 25-year period—1976–1999—was marked by less direct involvement. Government tended to play a more facilitatory role, creating the environment on which an industrial base could be built and providing structures and support services for new and growing sectors such as tourism, international financial services and the informatics sector. At the level of stabilization policy, the choices facing governments involved, from time to time, cutting current services, raising taxes and borrowing from abroad.

This study examines the role of government and the changing structure of the government sector, and evaluates its performance during the 50-year period 1950–1999. The study engages in the traditional Freidman-Galbraith debate about the role of government and of the market. However, it relies on the reality and the facts. It adopts the approach of examining government's role and performance and draws its conclusions from that analysis and to that extent it uses a deductive rather than an inductive approach.

This study is particularly concerned with shifts in the role performed by the state as reflected in public finances and in economic performance generally. It examines the sources of revenue, the growth of revenue, the allocation of expenditure to different sectors and the effect on the economy of financing the deficit. It illustrates how the development of the government sector was constrained by the openness of the economy, by the large labor force, by the threat of unemployment and by changing philosophies of the public role of government, both domestically and internationally. It suggests how these affected the historical evolution of the budget. It describes the inherent possibilities for fiscally generated inflation and suggests a causal relationship between fiscal deficits and monetary aggregates. Modified models that incorporate phenomena such as small size, degree of openness and the level of development are used to analyze fiscal performance. It treats with the question of size both as a constraint in the early part of the period and later, with increasing technologies, as an opportunity at the turn of the century. Specific attention is paid to periods when significant changes in policy stances occurred or where there were significant changes in economic performance that were influenced by fiscal policy.

No attempt is made to provide quantifiable interpretations of government performance in terms of distributional effects. Though such effects are sometimes referred to in the analysis in terms of the delivery of services. Distributional issues are dealt with generally and are not measured. The main focus of the study is on macroeconomic outcomes. The study does not expand on the regulatory role of government, since it is intended to focus on public finance and not the public sector generally. However, it is clear that government as regulator performs an important role, particularly with respect to utilities, exchange controls and through the Central Bank, in relation to interest rate policy and monetary policy generally. These policy shifts and regulatory initiatives are designed to influence market outcomes. However, the language of the twenty-first century finds the term "regulation" unacceptable and has substituted terms such as "stability concerns," but these too reflect the modern-day admission of the imperfection of markets without explicitly admitting of such imperfections.

Generally, public regulation of the market's shortcomings takes the form of legislative or administrative action, for example, investor protection, trust legislation, wills and intestacy and several other forms of protective legislation. These are viewed in the literature as acceptable forms of regulation. There are, however, other areas which are viewed as less acceptable. Price control is such an area. The fact that the latter device was little used in the 1980s and 1990s in Barbados may well be a recognition of its inefficiency as a regulatory device. However, since the impact of the regulatory role of government is difficult to quantify, it has not been given an important place in the analysis, more especially since the study emphasizes public finance management rather than regulation.

Data are obtained from various government publications.[7]

## CONCLUSION

Toward the end of the twentieth century and at the beginning of the twenty-first century, global trends such as removal of protection and liberalization of markets  contributed to increased vulnerability of small states. These challenges can, in due course, have implications for decisions about regional cooperation as small states seek to cushion themselves from the competitive power of Europe, North America and similar powerful states. The rules of the game heavily favor large countries which can benefit from significant economies of scale. The past 50 years will therefore be no predictor of the next 50. Economic alliances with other trade blocs will therefore be a necessity if small states such as Barbados are to sustain themselves or have sufficient resources to meet their goals. It will also be important to convince the international community that special recognition will need to be given to small countries in the context of international negotiations, for irrespective of the time given for small states to adjust to the challenges of liberalization and globalization, at the end of it, small states will still be small.

### NOTES

1. Local government in Barbados was abolished in 1965.

2. Deficits of the local government were financed by the central government.

3. Inaccessibility of data, differing fiscal years and the danger of double counting make the consolidation of revenue and expenditure for the total public sector very difficult.

4. As evidenced in the establishment of the Barbados Development Bank in 1969, The Insurance Corporation of Barbados in 1978 and the Barbados National Bank in 1979.

5. Some of the major government projects of the past two decades were the Hilton Hotel, the Barbados National Bank, the Insurance Corporation of Barbados, Heywoods, the Barbados Mills, the Pine Hill Dairy and the Arawak Cement Plant.

6. Statements from budget speeches suggest these goals.

7. The main sources of data are published in the Central Bank of Barbados and the Government Statistical Services. Statistics on the government sector are presented using international standards as set out in the *Manual on Government Finance Statistics*. The essential difference between the statistics reported by government and by the Central Bank of Barbados relate to the treatment of the Water Works Department and Post Office expenditure, which are excluded. Also, amortization payments are excluded from expenditures. All government statistics are on a fiscal year basis—April 1 to March 31. Reference to any year with respect to government accounts in the tables or text means the fiscal year ending March 31 of the following year. All other years are calendar years. All numbers are in Barbados dollars unless otherwise indicated. Numbers are revised from year to year. Consequently, there may be slight differences in the numbers published on a particular year compared with numbers published earlier by the same source. Every effort has been made to publish the most recently revised numbers.

**2**

---

# Theoretical Background and Constraints on Fiscal Policy

## INTRODUCTION
This chapter discusses the literature on public finance with special reference to small countries, but concentrates on issues related to expenditure, taxation, debt, financing and stabilization policies. It examines constraints such as small size, population density and stage of development and posits that despite disadvantages, some benefits can accrue from small size such as greater coordination, flexibility and better timing and sequencing. It offers varying definitions of openness and evaluates the implication for the management of public finances by small states of the opening of borders, of globalization, liberalization of markets and the disappearance of barriers to trade and investment.

Aggregate demand is normally given by the expression

$$Y = C+I+G+X-M$$

and national income by

$$Y = C+S+T$$

Therefore,

$$S+T = I+G+X-M.$$

Since voluntary savings are not likely to equal intended investment plus net exports at a level of income or aggregate demand that ensures stabilization, fiscal policy must therefore adjust budgets, taxes and expenditure, such that aggregate demand will utilize production capacity, without generating excess demand, inflation or balance of payment difficulties. In terms of stabilization policy, the level of taxation is intended to influence the level of consumption expenditure while the choice of different types of taxation is intended to influence consumer choice.

However, the overarching objective of government is economic development. In his seminal work on economic planning, Arthur Lewis (1969) noted that when fiscal policy is viewed as a means of achieving economic development and saving and investment is the key to such development, then the central problem in achieving rapid economic development is to determine the process by which a community that was previously saving and investing a small proportion of national income is transformed into an economy where voluntary saving is substantially increased.

## THEORIES OF PUBLIC EXPENDITURE

The modern approach to public finance starts from the assumption that the government wishes to maximize individual social welfare function in which social welfare is an increasing function of individual utilities (Newbery and Stern, 1987). Also, government expenditure plays a key role in the process of improvement in the standard of living and in raising per capita revenue, but is subject to several constraints.

Empirical studies on the relationship between public finances and economic growth differ in explanations of the role of public finances. Studies by Wagner (1958) were aimed at explaining the growth in public expenditures by looking at the growth of national income. Preoccupation with the importance of government in influencing the growth process Rubinson (1977) and Grossman (1988) seemed to focus on the reverse causality, that is, the extent to which government expenditures influenced economic growth. Other studies followed this approach, some focusing on the specific aspects of government spending that influence economic growth. For example, Diamond (1989) found that expenditure on social capital such as health, housing and welfare has a significant impact on growth in the short run. Other studies seek to explain the determinants of economic growth and focus on public finances as only one of several other factors that influence economic growth (Landau, 1986). More recent studies have focused on the impact of public finances on economic development rather than economic growth, defining economic growth as just one aspect of economic development (Smith and Wahba, 1997).

A common trend in government expenditures is the increasing demand for public goods as countries develop. Complex economies have greater demands for roads, airports, harbors, communications systems and other public goods. Increasingly in the 1990s, as management of public finances and as securitization of debt became more common, some of the services that formerly tended to be the preserve of governments were provided by the private sector. This led to a change in the perception that a public good has to be provided by a public institution.

## THEORIES OF TAXATION

For small developing countries, theories of taxation also require some modification. Generally the objectives of taxation are to raise funds to finance government expenditure, to restrain or reduce spending on goods and services by the private sectors, to effect some substitution in spending by consumers or to effect some redistribution in income. Some writers divide the tax effects into their impact on resources and their impact on incentives. The first is concerned with the effect on the transfer of purchasing power from households or enterprises to government. The second is concerned with the effect of taxes on the gain or penalty from engaging in a particular activity. For example, a progressive income tax with rising marginal rates increases the likelihood that risk-taking will be discouraged.

The incidence of taxation does tend to rise with the increase in per capita income. Comparisons among countries at different levels of per capita income generally show higher shares of government expenditure and of tax revenue in higher income countries. In developing countries one of the objectives of taxation that tends to lead to higher incidences of tax is the desire of governments to obtain sufficient government savings to finance capital formation.

In the late 1990s, the area of corporate taxation, particularly international corporate tax, became a topic of international interest. In the past, the national rate of tax was seen as a matter to be determined by each particular country. By the end of the century, because of the international movement of capital, there is now international interest in relative rates of national corporate tax. This interest extends also to choice of the tax base, capital cost allowances, depreciation systems and inflation adjustments.

International discussions have tended in the 1990s to emphasize the integration of personal and corporate taxation. The purist view is that individual tax rates and corporate tax rates should not differ and that to ensure this corporations should declare and pay profits over to shareholders who should then be taxed at the individual rate of tax.

Greater dialogue at the international level has centered around trade and tariffs. Rules of the General Agreement on Trade and Tariffs (GATT) have given way to WTO rules. However, many of the same issues recur. Their rules relate to the level of protective tariffs that countries should be permitted to impose on imported goods, and on the level of incentives that countries are permitted to offer to domestic producers. This has been accompanied by the introduction in many countries of nontax barriers and other phytosanitary rules that effectively keep several products out of developed markets. However, for the most part, similar rules do not exist in developing countries, with the result that several products produced in developed countries and that cannot be sold there, because of quality concerns, find their way into developing countries.

## THEORIES OF FINANCING AND DEBT MANAGEMENT

Theories of financing and of debt management tend to be very similar for developed and developing countries, but with respect to external financing there are some differences. In addition to the financing of public spending by way of the regular tax system, the issue of domestic debt, and the issuing of foreign debt are often resorted to when governments are unable to generate sufficient government savings to finance capital formation and to accelerate development. Indeed this is the norm.

However, a government's debt strategy must be supported by internal policies that are consistent if the strategy is to be sustainable. Assumption of debt has significant benefits for accelerated development but also carries economic and social costs. In addition, factors such as credit worthiness and solvency are important constraints on a country's debt strategy, and are important for some developing countries, more especially for their strategies for foreign borrowing. Other factors that impose constraints on borrowing are inflation and output growth. Hence, fiscal consistency implies that overall borrowing is in tandem with macroeconomic targets.

While the faster growth of an economy can help to reduce the debt burden by lowering the debt-output ratio or by slowing it down, interest payments on past debt, particularly where debts carry variable rates in a high interest rate scenario, can have a countervailing impact through consequential increases in debt service costs as higher real interest rates increase the debt burden. Faster growth, however, reduces debt-output ratios over time.

In attempting any analysis of external adjustment, it is therefore important to take into account the noninterest current account of the balance of payments as well as the interplay between real interest rates and real output growth.

The work of Wijnbergen is very instructive. Wijnbergen (1989) cautions about permitting the real interest rate to exceed the real rate of growth of the economy. If the real interest rate exceeds the real growth rate of the economy, he argues, the debt-output ratio rises; if it falls short of it, the ratio declines. He observes that if the real interest rate exceeds the real growth rate by a substantial margin, the debt dynamics term contributes significantly to increases in the debt-output ratio, limiting the room for noninterest current deficits. He argues that solvency and credit worthiness are therefore the two main considerations in managing external debt, and that to remain solvent, a country should not plan expenditures higher in discounted value terms than its current (discounted) future income minus its initial debt.

He notes that while borrowing should be well-planned and internally consistent, keeping a low debt-resource ratio is not necessarily a preferred option. Since the debt-resource ratio is a weighted average of the debt-output and debt-export ratios, the appropriateness of its debt resource ratio will depend on the growth rates of the borrowing country and its trading partners. It is this author's view that this is particularly so in countries that depend on tourism, as does Barbados. Another factor that influences growth is the elasticity of demand for the borrowing country's exports with respect to income in the countries to which it exports. Developing countries exporting primary products with low income elasticities of demand find it difficult to increase their export earnings at rates sufficient to fund desired borrowing, and so are often forced to restrict borrowing to below needed levels.

## STABILIZATION THEORIES

A consistent matching program of internal adjustment entails a set of policies to bring about a public and private surplus of savings over investment that matches the current account target. When a strategy of high growth is being pursued, it must be within the limits of solvency and credit worthiness. It is therefore important that the public sector contributes directly toward the necessary improvement in the savings surplus, or deficit reduction if internal stability is to be achieved. Ideally, a country should aim for a current account surplus and for high output growth so as to channel expenditure into productive, trade-oriented capital accumulation.

Higher investment, particularly in areas such as construction and wholesale and retail, invariably increases the aggregate demand for home goods and this puts upward pressure on the real exchange rate. That could crowd exports out and jeopardize credit worthiness by further diverting production from traded goods.

The formulation of an appropriate growth strategy therefore starts with a decision on what current account deficit is sustainable, borrowing of amounts that are consistent with solvency and credit worthiness, while making internal adjustments to ensure that additional borrowing goes for investment and output growth.

## THE FISCAL DEFICIT AND SAVINGS SURPLUS

While reduction of the fiscal deficit to levels consistent with the macroeconomic targets ensures that the fiscal policy is sustainable and that fiscal crises, high inflation, or escalating interest payments will not jeopardize the achievement of these targets, it does not guarantee that the targets can or will be achieved. The achievement depends on two major factors. First, there is a need for the private sector to generate enough surplus of private savings over private investments for the economy to achieve its external targets, given the fiscal deficit. Secondly, this surplus must be achieved at high enough levels of investment to meet output growth targets given the public program.

The central question is whether external restraint and the requirements for consistency in the fiscal deficit leave enough room for public and private investment and for satisfactory output growth. It is therefore important that the external balance and the output growth be reconciled and that there is no inherent conflict.

The interaction between fiscal policy and private savings and investment decisions is therefore crucial. A critical factor also is determining whether the structure of the economy is such that the private sector runs a surplus at high levels of savings and investment or at low levels. Wijnbergen (1989) observes that if the surplus is achieved by increasing savings or at the expense of sustained levels of investment cutbacks for given private savings rates, the external adjustment suppresses output growth.

Fiscal policy can directly influence the net private savings surplus through real interest-rate-based crowding out. High real interest rates slow private investment, thus slowing output growth, but other fiscal instruments can prevent such a slowdown in two ways. One is to shield private investment from the effect of high real interest rates. Another is through investment incentives, tax measures and credit policies.

Lower fiscal deficits for given interest rates and higher interest rates for given deficits both have welfare costs, the first in terms of cutbacks in government spending and the second through higher costs of operation of businesses and higher costs of servicing outstanding obligations. However, a properly designed adjustment program should include some of each in order to minimize the overall welfare costs.


## PUBLIC INVESTMENT

Public investment is important for offsetting some of the crowding out of private investment that results from fiscal deficits, since it can be used to shift government's expenditure from consumption to investment. Public investment, especially infrastructure, often stimulates rather than replaces private investment. Wijnbergen (1989) argues that empirical analysis on some countries (e.g., Turkey) shows that high real interest rates restrained private consumption more than private investment and that heavy public investment more than picked up the slack, allowing output growth to be sustained.

Cutting public investment reduces output growth, which in turn reduces the private sector's savings surplus. When this occurs, fiscal deficits and thus public investment often need to be cut further in order to maintain external balance, thus slowing growth even further. This is a very important outcome for small countries for which balance of payments equilibrium is essential to maintaining exchange rate stability.

Wijnbergen (1989) argues that if expenditure cuts come solely from government expenditure a given cutback in real interest rate requires a cut in the fiscal deficit of significant size to maintain external balance. But with a significant percentage of cutbacks coming from public investment, the deficit would need to be reduced by a large percentage of GNP. The argument does not imply a blanket endorsement of ever-increasing public investment. He argues that stabilization programs relying on reductions in public investment can have high and long-term negative output effects through the mechanism demonstrated. These negative effects are added to those that may arise because of short-term macroeconomic problems.

He argues that high real rates in a growth-oriented adjustment program may sound like a contradiction in terms, since growth requires high investment, and high real interest rates clearly slow down investment. But high real rates may be necessary to ensure that a large enough private savings surplus is generated to assure that fiscal deficits and the targets for external balance are consistent. To make sure that most of the effect of the high real rates is shifted toward consumption rather than investment, a government can use investment incentives and tax measures to deflect the impact of high real interest rates away from investment.

Public investment can do much to sustain growth, and cutting it excessively will jeopardize that goal. However, where the scope for balance of payments stability is being threatened, countries will have no option but to slow down.

## CONSTRAINTS ON PUBLIC FINANCES

### Small Size

Small size is important in explaining the rate at which expenditure increases, since small countries have high administrative costs per head of population.[1] Although there are obvious losses in small countries, for example, in constructing harbors, airports, holding foreign exchange reserves, financing universities and maintaining consulates and embassies abroad, compensating advantages of small size exist, such as greater coordination and flexibility in government. The Caribbean economist Lloyd Best (1971) suggests that factors such as timing, sequencing and manipulation are important weapons open to the small economy and that these can often offset some of the disadvantages of size.

The size of the government sector tends to increase over time. This is an international trend. For example, between 1970 and 1980 the size of government rose from 0.5 to 0.7 in Germany, from 0.6 to 1.0 in Sweden and from 0.40 to 0.55 in the United Kingdom, stabilizing or declining in the 1980s (Rosen and Weinberg, 1997).

In the United States, government expenditures grew sharply between 1970 and 1975 before declining over the rest of the period. In Japan, government expenditure grew from less than 25% of private consumption expenditure to 1970 to 36% in 1980, then stabilizing in the 1980s. Among developing countries, governments grew significantly during the period 1970–1990. Industrialized countries tended to devote a greater share of government expenditure to transfers and subsidies. On a capitalized basis the share of transfers and subsidies range from a low of roughly one-third in Iran, Ecuador, Korea and Venezuela to one-half in France, Germany, Greece, Japan, Sweden, United Kingdom and United States. For Barbados in the 1980s this accounted for approximately 20% of current expenditure.

## Openness
Closely allied to the problem of size is that of openness, both in the cultural and communications sense and in relation to trade. In a general sense, the influence of world opinion and social values and standards of welfare in metropolitan countries exert pressure on governments to ensure that high levels of social services are delivered domestically.

Many writers, for example, William Demas (1965) have noted these characteristics and suggested that the alternatives open to small economies are much more narrowly circumscribed than those open to large economies. However, in the 1990s these views have been sharply modified as technological changes have diminished some of the barriers of distance and accelerated the speed of learning. As economies have become more open and more liberalized, the barrier of small size has in some ways become less important, particularly in light of the spectacular success (despite setbacks) of the East Asian Tigers.

Various attempts have been made to measure openness as indicated by trade patterns. Other measures of openness have been tried. Lotz and Morss (1967) define openness as the ratio of imports plus exports to GNP.

In light of the current trends toward liberalization of markets, freer movement of capital, faster speed of information flows and improved communication and transportation, some of the disadvantages of small size are being eroded and openness now needs to be further redefined. However, the trend toward mergers and acquisitions and the proliferation of takeovers suggests other disadvantages are surfacing, and present a new competitive challenge for small open economies in an environment of liberalization, this time because of the breakdown in barriers. Ideally, new definitions of small size need therefore to include considerations of the size of the corporate sector, average firm size and possibly the extent and structure of transnational ownership.

## International Trends
A significant factor in the current literature on the role of government is the tendency to ignore the fact that many developing countries today may

be at the stage where  governments in industrialized countries found themselves 30–50 years ago.  The characteristics that they exhibited then in terms of expanding government sector's direct involvement in the provision of subsidies and similar incentives that  helped industrialized countries to develop, are today condemned as inappropriate solutions for developing countries.  There often is insufficient recognition that developed countries tried these remedies successfully 30–50 years ago and therefore should appreciate their relevance for developing countries today, even though they may no longer be relevant to developed countries themselves. There is instead, a tendency to universalize solutions without sufficient appreciation of current differences.  There is a presumption that the current remedies for large developed countries should be the same for small developing countries.  This is a challenge for developing countries in an age where demands for a level playing field, particularly in regard to subsidies and support, do not take these current differences or these facts of history into account.

## OVERVIEW OF BARBADOS' PUBLIC FINANCE PERFORMANCE

Barbados is a small island of 166 square miles (430 square kilometers) situated in the Caribbean sea.  It is the most easterly of these islands with a population in 1997 of 264,900 persons.  The island was a former British colony and obtained independence in 1966.  It is part of a regional common market arrangement, termed CARICOM.  Per capita income in 1999 was US$7,746, among the higher incomes of  developing countries.

The social welfare function as reflected in expenditure on the delivery of services was most significant in the first 25 years of the period under study. Data for Barbados suggest that income per head grew fairly steadily over the first 25 years of the period  (see Table 2.1) and that spending grew faster than GDP.  Income per head grew 6.0% per annum and real GDP 5.0% per annum.  In the second half of the century, as Barbados became more developed and income per head rose, government's share in GDP tended to rise and the cost of administration per head of population grew faster as new services were added.  In the last quarter of the twentieth century income per capita accelerated and GDP toward the end of 2000 was approaching US$8,000 per capita.

The importance of small size is borne out by the case of Barbados, since administrative costs are high, accounting for about 17.9% of total expenditure in 1950, rising to 20.1% of total expenditure in 1997. Data for the period do indeed show that increased population density during the period was matched by an increasing share of social service expenditure, but as the population achieved greater self-sufficiency, this ratio declined.[2] During this same period current expenditure on social services rose and then declined, from 36% of total spending in 1950 to 57% in 1976 but declined to 14.5% in 1997, reflecting the rising level of self sufficiency of the population.

Size tended to become less significant during the second half of the period and in the last 25 years, negotiating abilities, ability to find niche markets through identification of new areas of development and diplomatic and other skills combined with technological developments to help in the country's efforts to maintain its competitive position.

The factor of small size however, continued to be a major issue for the finance of the Barbadian economy. Without simplifying the case (since there were other factors such as competitiveness that explained this phenomenon) the most successful entrepreneurs tended to be those who could overcome small size by expanding into overseas markets. This suggests that if the barrier of small size can be overcome by outward-looking activities, then the prospects of viability increase. Indeed, the small proportion of industry and manufacturing in GDP may be a result of the diseconomies of size in these sectors and of inward-looking approaches to development. Despite the argument that suggests that size can be overcome, many services bear a high charge per capita because of diseconomies of size. These arguments involve diseconomies of scale in water services and public utilities and particularly diseconomies of operating economic services for a small population. Some of these costs therefore had to be absorbed by government.

Small size has its advantages in facilitating commitment to common goals. There is empirical evidence from the 1990s, in the form of a social compact between government, labor unions and the private sector, that small size can be an important factor in developing a cooperative approach to problem solving and in enlisting support of key economic groups. In a small environment, moral suasion is more effective. This became evident in the early 1990s in difficult economic times when foreign exchange conservation, control of consumer spending and wage restraint were important factors in alleviating pressures on the economy that would otherwise have been more debilitating, but whose remediation required the cooperation of the consuming public.

**Table 2.1**

**Government's Share in Gross Domestic Product, 1950–1998**

| Period | Govt's share in GDP | % change per annum | $ million GDP in current prices | Per capita GDP current prices | % change per annum in per capita income | Real Growth Rate per annum |
|--------|------|------|------|------|------|------|
| 1950 | 9.5 | | 54.5 | 277.0 | .. | 3.9 |
| 1955 | 8.7 | 14.5 | 102.7 | 451.0 | 0.7 | 3.9 |
| 1960 | 9.7 | 27.7 | 125.5 | 538.0 | -4.2 | -13.7 |
| 1965 | 12.4 | 10.6 | 158.2 | 669.0 | 5.1 | -7.0 |
| 1970 | 14.7 | -5.7 | 289.7 | 1,209.0 | 17.0 | 9.7 |
| 1975 | 15.0 | -4.4 | 700.6 | 2,847.0 | 9.0 | -1.9 |
| 1980 | 14.2 | -5.4 | 1,535.8 | 6,157.0 | 28.1 | 4.4 |
| 1985 | 15.8 | 10.7 | 2,180.7 | 8,485.0 | 4.6 | 1.1 |
| 1990 | 18.5 | 6.9 | 2,965.2 | 11,022.0 | -1.1 | -3.3 |
| 1995 | 17.2 | -4.1 | 3,136.6 | 11,863.0 | 7.4 | 2.9 |
| 1998 | 17.0 | -0.6 | 3,875.2 | 14,568.0 | 5.2 | 2.5 |

*Sources:* Government of Barbados Economic Reports; Government Statistical Service, abstract of statistics; Central Bank of Barbados, annual statistical digests.

International consensus seems, however, to stress the disadvantages of size. In Barbados, factors such as timing and sequencing have proved very difficult to overcome in achieving greater speed in implementation. The mileage gained from these techniques when applied to public finance has proven to be very limited.

The country tends to aspire to a standard of social service similar to that obtaining in larger and more developed countries. Social services were provided mostly by government and other nongovernment organizations and, in some cases, surpassed the level of social services provided by many developed countries. However, the greatest constraint which openness imposed on the public expenditures was in the provision of foreign exchange that persistently dogged the national economic effort.

If openness is measured by the ratio of imports to GDP, by this measure, the Barbadian economy was quite open.[3] The ratio of imports to GDP fluctuated around an average of 70% of GDP rising as high as 82.7%. Using the Lotz-Morss measure of openness—imports plus exports to GDP, the evidence suggests a declining degree of openness. The economy appears to have been most open between 1963 and 1968 when the ratio of imports plus exports to GDP averaged 112%. This compares in 1997 with a ratio of 71.6% indicating that, as measured by this index, the economy became less open. Because of the importance of tourism in the second half of the period 1975–1997, the measure of openness was modified to include a measure for tourism. Openness is shown to have increased using measures of openness that include tourism. While international trends and liberalization of economies call for a redefinition of openness, data constraints limit the extent to which such redefinitions of openness can be practically measured.[4]

Persistently high levels of unemployment impose another constraint on the public finances. This constraint has been the bane of many governments who, from time to time, have yielded to pressures to deliver higher levels of employment with dire consequences for fiscal outcomes. While the rate of unemployment growth has been contained for most of the period under study, this rate remained high, for much of the period. It has resulted in emphasis being placed, from time to time, on short-term labor-engaging activities rather than on long-term, structural change. The burden of unemployment therefore has a potential for becoming self-perpetuating, particularly since political considerations of providing employment do bear weight in arguments for long-term structural change where limited resources force the country to choose one of these alternatives. The high ratio of expenditure on road works and infrastructural development that is evident from time to time is partly indicative of this problem. Some of this type of spending reflects political priorities rather than economic necessities and is sometimes undertaken to alleviate the high level of unemployment.

Generally, however, fiscal management of the Barbadian economy was conservative. It focused on public well-being and economic growth as simultaneous objectives.

**NOTES**

1.  Studies differ over the definition of administration.

2.  In 1950 population density in Barbados was 1,185 persons per square  mile, and by 1975 this had risen to 1,486 per square mile, and by 1998 to 1,602.

3.  Hinrichs (1965) puts forward the hypothesis that government's revenue share in GNP is positively related to the share of imports in GNP in an open economy and that M/Y is measure of openness.

4.  Import duties account for one-third of revenue (compared with 1% in the United States).

# 3

---

# The Level and Pattern of Public Spending

## INTRODUCTION
This chapter establishes norms against which planners may evaluate the adequacy of expenditures. It looks at the implications for the budget of socially determined expenditures and discusses the merits of advocating "smaller government" as a prescription for improved fiscal management of small economies. In examining the relationship between the level of services and the rate of economic growth, public spending is placed against the background of the objectives of the public sector. The nexus between expenditure and growth is examined. That analysis is informed by the view of Diamond (1989) that, based on the contribution of government expenditure to the growth performance of a sample of developing countries, that the aggregate level of public spending had not exerted a major influence on growth. However, he noted that in using disaggregated data (expressing each item in terms of its share of GDP) that social capital expenditure on health, housing and welfare seemed to have a significant impact on growth in the short run. This study also analyzes the elasticities of expenditures with respect to income and, assesses the overall impact of public spending on income distribution as far as data permit. The part played by personal emoluments in government's expenditure and pressures to improve levels of employment in the context of budget constraints are also given some emphasis.

## JUDGING THE ADEQUACY OF SPENDING
Unless government services are seen as another specialized service in a "generally technologically determined production function," then it is

necessary to establish some norms against which planners compare and judge the adequacy of the pattern and level of government spending. It is equally important to establish the nature of the forces that govern the determination of government expenditure. This bears on the question of whether there is some optimal proportion of government expenditure that should be devoted to certain activities relative to others. Essentially, this would appear to depend on the priorities of government. However, there are initial conditions (e.g., the level of development and the standard of living) that impact on the proportion of the budget devoted to certain activities.

In Barbados, a large percentage of the services of government are socially related and are influenced by the changing social framework of the society (see Tables 3.1 and 3.2). These changes are a reflection of underlying changes in the structure of the economy and the stage of development. Expenditure tends to increase annually. However, toward the last decade of the 1990s changing perceptions of the state challenged the validity of Wagner's law of increasing public expenditures. Wagner's law, in reverse, was espoused as a criterion for good government. That is, "smaller government" became a byword and was seen as a means of improving long-term economic growth prospects and of ensuring the viability of developing countries, both large and small. How much this was influenced by multinational corporations is difficult to ascertain, but it certainly redounded to their benefit, as is evident from the several privatizations in Latin America and the large inflows of equity capital that accompanied initiatives to achieve smaller government and to ensure commercialization in the delivery of services formerly provided by governments.

## EXPENDITURE AND OUTPUT

Two questions are often raised concerning the relationship between the rate of economic growth and the share of government expenditure. Firstly, does this positive correlation imply mutual causation? That is, does increased national product result from higher public spending, or is increased public spending a result of higher incomes and, consequently, larger revenues. Secondly, is the level of services consistent with the rate of increase in national product? As one economist observed "the goals, institutions and behavior patterns in the Caribbean defeat attempts to match ends and means." In Barbados, public expenditure on social services grew at an average annual rate of 16.8% between 1950 and 1976, higher than the average rate of growth of GDP.

**Table 3.1**
**Government Expenditure by Function, 1950–1998**
**$ million**

| Period | General services | Social services | Economic services | Debt charges | Total |
|---|---|---|---|---|---|
| 1950 | 2.0 | 4.0 | 5.1 | 0.2 | 11.2 |
| 1955 | 3.2 | 6.7 | 5.4 | 0.3 | 18.2 |
| 1960 | 5.5 | 10.3 | 13.2 | 0.7 | 30.5 |
| 1965 | 6.7 | 18.7 | 15.1 | 2.7 | 42.7 |
| 1969 | 21.0 | 38.0 | 15.6 | 4.4 | 79.0 |
| 1970 | 21.5 | 52.4 | 20.4 | 4.3 | 99.5 |
| 1975 | 44.2 | 117.2 | 46.7 | 13.7 | 220.1 |
| 1976 | 42.1 | 141.3 | 75.2 | 14.2 | 272.9 |
| 1980 | 99.6 | 309.5 | 123.6 | 30.5 | 530.8 |
| 1985 | 161.4 | 375.8 | 155.2 | 69.8 | 769.2 |
| 1990 | 213.1 | 634.6 | 217.4 | 132.2 | 1,197.7 |
| 1995 | 253.3 | 578.1 | 172.5 | 189.8 | 1,194.5 |
| 1997 | 302.6 | 748.7 | 206.3 | 201.8 | 1,508.8 |
| 1998 | 286.0 | 775.0 | 310.6 | 218.9 | 1,589.7 |

*Note*: Columns do not sum to the total because the column titled "other" is not included.

*Sources*: Estimates of Government's revenue and expenditure; Central Bank of Barbados, annual statistical digests.

**Table 3.2**
**Total Expenditure by Category, 1957–1998**
**$ million**

| Period | Education | Health | Housing | Roads & Transportation | Agriculture |
|---|---|---|---|---|---|
| 1957 | 3.7 | 2.3 | 1.1 | 5.4 | 1.4 |
| 1960 | 4.2 | 3.2 | 1.1 | 9.0 | 1.9 |
| 1965 | 8.7 | 6.3 | 0.4 | 4.9 | 1.8 |
| 1969 | 17.0 | 12.1 | 2.9 | 7.9 | 2.8 |
| 1970 | 21.2 | 16.1 | 5.9 | 11.6 | 3.5 |
| 1975 | 50.1 | 34.9 | 9.1 | 24.3 | 8.8 |
| 1980 | 111.8 | 66.6 | 22.2 | 67.7 | 18.6 |
| 1985 | 158.6 | 100.2 | 32.2 | 90.1 | 26.3 |
| 1990 | 285.0 | 165.8 | 66.5 | 123.2 | 35.8 |
| 1995 | 241.5 | 161.1 | 60.1 | 77.9 | 31.3 |
| 1997 | 276.4 | 167.9 | 101.7 | 93.2 | 38.7 |
| 1998 | 327.6 | 185.0 | 102.1 | 164.4 | 42.6 |

*Sources*: Estimates of Government's revenue and expenditure; Central Bank of Barbados, annual statistical digests.

Different expenditures may be expected to have different effects on growth. The objectives of budgets, based on budget presentations were mainly the upgrading of living standards, the reduction of unemployment and the encouragement of industry. The pattern of government spending therefore tended to reflect the objectives of government. Direct provision of services was the preference of government. Efforts to upgrade the standard of living were reflected in expenditure on social services through transfers and subsidies and through the provision of social infrastructure (see Tables 3.1, 3.2 and 3.3). The welfare implication of providing services directly differs from that of providing finance for the provision of services.

Consequently, the share of government spending in direct provision when compared with that of subsidies and transfers produces different results. Generally, it is claimed (Rosen and Weinberg, 1997) that government production of services may be less efficient than private production. However, direct provision of services was the most frequently used approach.

**Table 3.3**
**Share of Expenditure, 1957–1998**
%

| Period | Share of Education | Share of Health | Share of Housing | Share of Roads | Share of Agriculture |
|--------|--------------------|-----------------|------------------|----------------|----------------------|
| 1957 | 15.2 | 9.5 | 4.5 | 22.2 | 5.8 |
| 1960 | 13.8 | 10.5 | 3.6 | 29.5 | 6.2 |
| 1965 | 20.4 | 14.8 | 0.9 | 11.5 | 4.2 |
| 1969 | 21.5 | 15.3 | 3.7 | 10.0 | 3.5 |
| 1970 | 21.3 | 16.2 | 5.9 | 11.7 | 3.5 |
| 1975 | 22.7 | 15.9 | 4.1 | 11.0 | 4.0 |
| 1976 | 22.3 | 14.3 | 3.3 | 16.9 | 4.1 |
| 1980 | 21.1 | 12.5 | 4.2 | 12.7 | 3.5 |
| 1985 | 20.6 | 13.0 | 4.2 | 11.7 | 3.4 |
| 1990 | 23.8 | 13.8 | 5.6 | 10.3 | 3.0 |
| 1993 | 24.6 | 13.6 | 3.7 | 6.6 | 2.6 |
| 1995 | 20.2 | 13.5 | 5.0 | 6.5 | 2.6 |
| 1997 | 21.4 | 11.3 | 7.2 | 6.6 | 2.6 |
| 1998 | 20.5 | 11.6 | 6.4 | 10.3 | 2.7 |

*Sources*: Estimates of Government's revenue and expenditure; Central Bank of Barbados, annual statistical digests.

Transfers to households, in the form of social security and welfare payments during the period 1950–1975, rose from 9.5% of total current expenditure in 1950 to 11.0% in 1975, and represented a relatively stable ratio for most of the period. However, expenditure on welfare services in the post-1964 period (which accounts for a large proportion of transfers to households) became increasingly important, absorbing the major proportion of expenditure. Expenditure on subsidies tended to decline as the standard of living rose, falling from $1.5 million in 1950 to $0.9 million in 1964. Separate data for subsidies are not available for the post-1964 period. Available data for the period 1981–1985 show a category titled "subsidies and transfers" accounting for 34.2% of current expenditure in 1981 and 27.1% in 1995. Though the absolute level was relatively high, a slight decline is observed for the period 1981–1995. This suggests that subsidies declined as the standard of living improved.

In the mid-1960s increased emphasis was placed on health and education, and heavy outlays made on social services and welfare. This continued into the 1980s and 1990s. Outlays on social services rose from 35.7% of spending in 1950, to 51.8% in 1976 and declined by 1997 to 49.6% (see Table 3.1), suggesting some of the targeted goals may have been reached. Within the category "social services," spending on health and education rose swiftly, later leveling off. Expenditure on education rose from 18% of total spending in 1950, to 22.3% in 1976 and was at 21.4% in 1997 (see Table 3.3). This category exhibited a high elasticity coefficient of 1.4 during the period 1950–1975 and a coefficient of 1.1 during the period 1976–1999.

Global data for the period 1953–1990 show the outlay on education by Barbados, at about 24% of GDP, comparing favorably with World Bank global estimates of expenditure in this category. A study by Rosen and Weinberg (1997) indicates that in most countries education accounts for 20–30% of government consumption expenditure. In Israel, Japan, Korea, the United States and Zimbabwe this figure is closer to 40%, and between 30% and 40% in most of Latin America. Lower levels of spending on education are evident in Bangladesh, Greece and India (between 10% and 20%).

Recognition of the need for technical education and computer literacy in schools, and the jarring realization that the 97.6% literacy rate of which Barbados had so long been proud was not sufficiently functional to take it into the new millennium, prompted a determination by government to shift a greater portion of its resources into the supply of education and training more relevant to the twenty-first century. Consequently, during the mid-

1990s the share of education in total spending rose sharply and in 1993 reached 24.6% of total expenditure, the highest level since the mid-1970s.

A pattern of rapid increases and slight slowing off is evident in the area of health. In health, expenditures rose from 10% of total current spending in 1950, and reached a high point in 1969 when it absorbed 23.3% of total expenditure and declined to 13.3% in 1997 (see Table 3.3). Spending on health displayed the highest elasticity coefficient (1.47) in the 1950–1975 period but declined to 1.02 in the last quarter of the century (see Tables 3.4 and 3.5). This may have been indicative of the fact that much of the infrastructural development in the health sector had taken place prior to the 1976 period, but may indicate some shifting of responsibilities toward greater private sector provision of health care. Similar comparative global data on expenditure and health show that spending on health was highest in Western Europe (Rosen and Weinberg, 1997), where it ranged from 20% in France to between 25% and 30% in Sweden and up to 35% in Germany and the United Kingdom. The share of government consumption expenditure devoted to medical care was much lower in the United States (less than 10% during the 1970s and 1980s) and less than 5% in Japan. This compares with Bangladesh, Colombia, Ecuador and India, where it is less than 10% of defence spending. Expenditure by Barbados in the last 25 years shows some slippage from 15.9% in 1975 to 11.6% in 1998.

Data are not available on the percentage of total medical care by government as compared with the private sector, but unofficial estimates suggest that this is quite high and in the 1990s would compare favorably with the 80% by governments in Germany, Sweden and the United Kingdom. This compares with 40% in France and 8–10% in the United States (Rosen and Weinberg, 1997). Using GDP as a proxy for economic development, data for 1950–1975 show a positive correlation between government expenditure and GDP. When government expenditure is regressed on GDP the relationship is significant. The coefficient of determination is 0.82. The total responsiveness of expenditure to GDP was estimated at 0.90 (see Table 3.4). The high expenditure elasticity is partly attributable to the rise in per capita income and the improved level of development.

During the second half of the period, that is, 1976–1998, similar regression results show a continued responsiveness to GDP. The coefficient of determination is 0.99 and the elasticity of total expenditure with respect to

GDP is 1.09. This indicates that during the latter part of the period expenditure tended to move more in tandem with output than in the earlier period.

**Table 3.4**
**Log Linear Regression Results, 1950–1975, Government Expenditure Regressed on GDP**

|                      | $R^2$ | Elasticity coefficient | T statistic | DW statistic |
|----------------------|-------|------------------------|-------------|--------------|
| Total expenditure    | 0.82  | 0.90                   | 10.58       | .73          |
| Education            | 0.98  | 1.41                   | 10.07       | 1.28         |
| Health               | 0.97  | 1.47                   | 10.07       | 1.5          |
| Social services      | 0.82  | 1.02                   | 10.67       | 1.75         |
| Economic services    | 0.75  | 1.66                   | 8.74        | 1.45         |
| General services     | 0.79  | 0.91                   | 9.67        | 1.58         |
| Capital expenditure  | 0.72  | 1.00                   | 8.04        | 1.09         |

**Table 3.5**
**Log Linear Regression Results, 1976–1998, Government Expenditure Regressed on GDP**

|                      | $R^2$ | Elas coeff | T Stat. | DW Stat. | Const |
|----------------------|-------|------------|---------|----------|-------|
| Total expenditure    | 0.99  | 1.09       | 39.83   | 1.15     | -1.74 |
| Education            | 0.95  | 1.11       | 19.7    | 1.17     | -3.47 |
| Health               | 0.98  | 1.02       | 29.98   | 2.11     | -3.13 |
| Social services      | 0.98  | 1.02       | 28.11   | 1.04     | -1.88 |
| Economic services    | 0.81  | 0.63       | 9.33    | 0.96     | -0.11 |
| General services     | 0.97  | 1.26       | 25.55   | 2.08     | -4.67 |
| Capital expenditure  | 0.58  | 0.71       | 5.42    | 0.81     | -0.49 |

The overall expenditure on social services such as health and education showed an elasticity coefficient of 1.4 in 1950–1975 (see Table 3.4) and 1.02 and 1.11 in 1976–1998 (see Table 3.5).

Varying problems surfaced from time to time in the management of public finances. These included excessive public sector wage bills, surplus numbers of government servants, cost pressures arising from revisions of public servants salaries, wage compression of top general workers' salaries and, toward the end of the century, the challenge of increasing productivity in the public service. (Increasing compression of top salaries was identified as a serious constraint on government's ability to attract and retain qualified personnel at the middle and higher levels.)

Initiatives at restructuring were informed by the changing role and public expectations of the state, and more especially by a recognition of the importance of the state as a primary provider of social welfare, with responsibility for improving the country's level of development, so that restructuring was initiated in this context. Coincident with measures for increasing productivity was the establishment of a poverty alleviation program. This underscored the emphasis on improving the standards of living and on income redistribution, and on maintaining the high per capita income of Barbados.

## PERSONAL EMOLUMENTS

The emphasis on reducing unemployment tended to explain the increasing level of spending on personal emoluments and the increasing number of persons employed in the public service. Government's share of the work force increased until 1992; rising from 13.7% in 1960, to 26.4% in 1976,[1] and falling to 16.2% by 1992, in response to stabilization measures. It remained fairly stable at 16.5% in 1996. Despite the increasing share of employment in government, the overall unemployment rate rose from 9.9% in 1960 to 15% in 1974, peaking at 26.2% in March 1993. It is suggested that the public sector was not able to expand sufficiently to take up the slack. However, in the post-1993 period unemployment dropped dramatically to 9.8% by December 1999.

Outlays on wages and salaries accounted for a significant portion of the budget, averaging 34.9% of expenditure between 1950 and 1975. By 1979 this ratio peaked again at 47.7% of current expenditure and by 1995 represented 40.1% of current expenditure, but had reached a low of 38.3% in 1992 during the structural adjustment period (see Table 3.6). As government's wage bill began to represent a substantially larger percentage of the total budget in the post 1991 period, a trade-off became necessary between increasing the average earnings of government workers and increasing the number of workers. This was not resolved until the structural adjustment period in 1992.

In the 1990s increasing attention was paid to public pay and employment shares, to the constraints these placed on the wage bill and on their share in public expenditures. Increases in wage rates tended to reduce the capacity of government to provide jobs. This was never more apparent than in fiscal year 19991/1992, when over 3,000 persons were laid off in the government service and salaries were cut by 8% in order to assist government in correcting a severe fiscal situation.

## OTHER SERVICES

Expenditure on economic services rose slowly despite official emphasis on this sector.[2] Whereas in 1950 economic services had absorbed a large proportion of spending, by 1976 spending on this category had declined in importance relative to social services. Outlays on economic services fell from 45.5% of total spending in 1950 to 27.6% in 1976 and to 19.5% in 1997. The elasticity coefficient of expenditure on economic services with respect to GDP was 1.66 in 1950–1975 and 0.63 in the period 1976–1998.

Spending on roads, airports and harbors absorbed a large proportion of the expenditure. The share of spending on agriculture was stagnant and ranged between 2.5% and 6%. This contrasts strongly with its importance in GDP in the early period. (About-one quarter of GDP was contributed by agriculture in the period 1960–1967. Thereafter the share of agriculture in GDP declined and by 1997 accounted for only 4.9% of GDP.) The pattern of spending can therefore be summarized as giving high priority to social services, sometimes at the expense of economic services (see Table 3.6).

In the absence of data on income distribution, it is difficult to measure the incidence of government expenditure on income groups accurately. However, if the breakdown of expenditure by function is used as a guide, it is possible to estimate roughly the benefits of this expenditure.

Expenditure on economic services is assumed to benefit all equally and to the extent that it encouraged entrepreneurship tended to benefit the business sector particularly. Expenditure on education is also assumed to be unbiased in its application. No effort is made to discriminate against the higher income earners. For a short period when the economy was experiencing severe fiscal difficulties (1991–1993) consideration was given to resorting to market pricing for some government-provided services and to the delivery of some social services on a needs basis, but this was short-lived. Financial assistance for university education on a needs basis was also considered, but popular pressure forced government to review this despite the fact that high-income earners who benefitted were in a position to fund or partly fund their own education.

**Table 3.6**
**Wages, Transfers and Subsidies, 1950–1998**

| Period | Wages and salaries $ million | Wages and salaries as a % of total current expenditure | Subsidies and transfers $ million | Subsidies and transfers as a % of total current expenditure |
|---|---|---|---|---|
| 1950 | 3.4 | 45.0 | 2.2 | 22.0 |
| 1955 | 5.5 | 40.4 | 2.3 | 16.9 |
| 1960 | 8.0 | 37.0 | 4.7 | 21.8 |
| 1965 | 11.5 | 35.4 | .. | .. |
| 1970 | 38.9 | 46.8 | .. | .. |
| 1975 | 72.0 | 41.3 | .. | .. |
| 1979 | 150.3 | 47.8 | .. | .. |
| 1981 | 183.7 | 40.8 | 153.9 | 34.2 |
| 1985 | 266.8 | 42.6 | 266.8 | 42.6 |
| 1990 | 423.6 | 44.2 | 245.9 | 25.7 |
| 1992 | 360.3 | 38.3 | 231.7 | 24.6 |
| 1995 | 424.2 | 40.1 | 286.6 | 27.1 |

*Sources*: Government of Barbados Economic Report; Central Bank of Barbados, annual statistical digests.

The typical free-rider problem results from this approach, whereby benefits are extended to all irrespective of ability to pay. Theoretically, where benefits and costs are borne by different groups, this can result in some dissatisfaction, but while there have been some queries raised, principally by international financial institutions, this general approach continues to find acceptance at the national level.

Expenditure on social services remained geared to benefit the lower-level earners mostly and several of the welfare benefits were linked to minium levels of income. These transfers were negative taxes and tended to fall as income rose. Some social expenditures have secondary effects, for example, expenditures on education, health and transportation also tend to increase the overall efficiency of the economy through improved productivity levels and to that extent, not only benefit the recipients but the national economy.

Acceptance of the level of spending on education extended also to acceptance of the need for transfers and subsidies. However, the level of transfers per capita was far lower than in the United States and some countries in Western Europe, where entitlement programs and welfare programs represented substantial percentages of the budget.

Given the high level of expenditure on social services and the high benefit rate of these expenditures, it could be concluded that the greatest benefit of public spending accrued to those in the lower-income brackets and that expenditure tended to have a pro-poor bias and to that extent assisted in affecting some redistribution of incomes.

Indeed, in 1998, government set in motion a poverty eradication program and in 1999 created a Ministry of Social Transformation. Per capita income at the time of its establishment was around US$7,000, the second highest in the Caribbean Community and Common Market (CARICOM). However, toward the end of the decade there was a perception of widening disparities in income. This seemed to be associated with the highly successful development of the international business sector and an increasing number of foreign residents. It was accompanied by an increasingly high profile being given, first to the Ministry of Social Transformation and increased budget allocations for social expenditure related to poverty alleviation. The only available study of income distribution in Barbados, done over a period of time, spans the period 1951–1981 (Holder and Prescod, 1984). That study concluded, using taxable income, that inequality declined over the 1950s and 1970s and that the progressivity of the income tax structure was a major factor in the reduction of inequality of income. The writers concluded that over time the distribution of income within the lower income groups, although more unequal than overall, was better distributed as a result of wage and tax policies. However, subsequent studies on other countries show that increasing inequality of income appeared to be a world wide phenomenon in the post-1970 period. A publication by the World Institute for Development Research (Atkinson, 1999) notes a global increase in inequality of income. Countries cited include the US, where the trend was observed in the 1970s, the UK, most OECD countries and more especially New Zealand, Germany, Netherlands and France. In the UK case, the Gini coefficient rose by 10 percentage points from around 23% in 1977 to 33% in 1990. (The coefficient can vary from 0% when everyone has equal income to 100% when one person has all). In an article in the same journal (Jolly, 1999) observed that the gap between the rich and poor nations is now at its highest ever. For the period for which data were available, the Barbados situation appeared to show narrowing inequality up to 1980. However, despite the unavailability of data, it is unlikely that Barbados would have escaped the global trend of increasing inequality in the last two decades of the twentieth century.

Generally, the scope for management of the budget became quite limited as these social expenditures became institutionalized, partly in an effort to ensure that social services were maintained. Trade-offs were possible between one head of expenditure and another in an effort to keep within budgeted limits and some degree of compensation took place from year to year, expanding some categories in one year and contracting them in the next. This was more possible in those categories where spending was flexible. Economic services tended to be that category and the most flexible area of spending, and hence activities such as roadworks and transport, where costs were more variable, were subject to the greatest fluctuations and were dependent on the exigencies of the budget process.

## CONCLUSION

An evaluation of the period shows increasing emphasis on social expenditures beginning in the post independence era and continuing up to the early 1990s, just prior to the stabilization program of 1991–1992. However, during the stabilization program an important feature was the beginning of some consideration to provision of services on a needs basis and the estimation of economic costs. Efforts to introduce a greater element of personal contribution into education at University level were also resisted by many who argued for continued free education despite rising incomes and despite the financial distress which visited the University from time to time.

**NOTES**

1. Data were taken from the 1960 and 1970 censuses and the 1976 household survey.

2. Part of the reduced importance of economic services in the budget is accounted for by the establishment of several statutory boards that were intended to promote the advancement of specific sectors, for example, agriculture and industry.

**4**

# Capital and Development Spending

## INTRODUCTION

This chapter evaluates the contribution of capital spending and examines whether capital spending by government enhances productive capacity. The relationship between the capital budget and fixed capital formation and between development spending and capital investment is analyzed. Special emphasis is given to spending on infrastructural projects, particularly given the relatively low absorptive capacity of government with respect to funding during the early years of the period. Issues of access to project funding are also discussed. The costs and benefits of establishment of several off-budget statutory boards, their contribution to economic growth and their role in promoting accelerated development are also examined.

## CAPITAL SPENDING AND GROWTH

It is not possible to estimate accurately the extent to which government capital spending promoted economic growth in the 1950–1976 period, since it is the relationship between capital spending and the rate of growth of fixed capital formation (rather than GDP) that is important, and a complete series on the latter was not available. Capital formation relates to the rate of growth of investment in productive capacity and throws light on whether increased spending assisted productive capacity.

The remarkable growth of the East Asian newly industrialized economies, though apparently private-sector led, has shown that in reality, state intervention can be very important in achieving accelerated economic growth. This experience has been termed by some as market-friendly government intervention. Essentially it demonstrates that the direction that government intervention takes is crucial to the success of government's effort to achieve accelerated economic growth.

From the limited data available, whereas government's share in the flow of GDP doubled in the period 1950–1975, gross domestic capital formation rose one-third, suggesting a rate of capital formation slower than government's share in spending. In the second half of the period 1976–1998, government's share in GDP rose much more slowly, from 15.0% of GDP in 1975 to 17% of GDP in 1998 (see Table 4.1), while domestic gross capital formation almost tripled.

**Table 4.1**
**Capital Expenditure: Share in Total Expenditure, 1950–1998**
$ million

| Period | Capital Expenditure | Total Expenditure | Capital as a % of total expenditure |
|--------|--------------------|--------------------|------------------------------------|
| 1950 | 0.9 | 11.2 | 8.1 |
| 1955 | 4.7 | 18.2 | 25.6 |
| 1960 | 8.8 | 30.5 | 28.9 |
| 1963 | 9.6 | 27.0 | 35.5 |
| 1965 | 10.1 | 42.7 | 23.7 |
| 1970 | 15.8 | 99.5 | 15.9 |
| 1975 | 48.3 | 220.1 | 21.9 |
| 1980 | 138.8 | 530.8 | 26.1 |
| 1981 | 173.1 | 624.3 | 27.7 |
| 1985 | 146.1 | 769.2 | 19.0 |
| 1990 | 240.1 | 1,197.7 | 20.0 |
| 1995 | 135.5 | 1,194.5 | 11.3 |
| 1998 | 256.8 | 1,574.7 | 16.3 |

*Sources*: Government of Barbados Economic Report; Estimates of Government's revenue and expenditure; Central Bank of Barbados, annual statistical digests.

The capital budget, so-called, is not a true representation of government's capital spending, and is only a rough indicator of gross fixed capital formation of the public sector since much of government's capital projects are off-budget. However, capital spending grew at an annual average of 33.9% in current prices, and accounted for 8.1% of total spending in 1950 and 21.9% in 1975 and 16.3% in 1998. The 1960s were high points of capital spending and the early and mid-1990, low points. During the 1990s there were sharp cutbacks in capital spending, particularly during the 1991–1994 period when the share of capital spending in total spending fell to 9.9% in 1992, but by 1998 had again risen to 16.3% (see Table 4.1). Despite the official emphasis on development spending, the rate at which capital investment rose still fell below that required for rapidly accelerating economic growth and was sometimes traded off against stabilization imperatives. Different sectors predominated the budget in different periods; education in the 1970s and 1990; health in the 1980s and housing in the late 1970s, the late 1980s and in the 1990s (see Table 4.2). Capital spending on agriculture tended to be mostly below 10% of the budget but a significant proportion of the capital budget was devoted to road building, from time to time, particularly in the 1960s and again in the late 1990s (see Table 4.3).

## CAPITAL SPENDING ON INFRASTRUCTURAL PROJECTS

As with current expenditures a great deal of capital expenditure was spent on social infrastructure, schools, hospitals, and similar infrastructural developments. The bulk of capital expenditure on economic services financed the construction of the airport, the harbor and other physical infrastructure. However, the capacity of government to absorb new funds was limited by the level of technological development for part of the period. Indeed the country displayed low absorptive capacity for much of the period. This was a result of bottlenecks relating to skilled personnel, management ability and so on. The extent to which capital spending increased in the period 1950–1976 was partly attributable to improved capacity but this improvement was more evident during the 1980s and 1990s. Technical assistance from international agencies was increased in an effort to raise absorptive capacity and to improve the maximum domestic effort. The lower share of capital spending in the 1990s was more attributable to the pressures of economic stabilization than to constraints of absorptive capacity.

Table 4.2

Capital Expenditure by Major Heads:  Social Services, 1950–1998

$ million

| Period | Educa-tion | Education as a % of total capital expenditure | Health | Health as a % of total capital expenditure | Housing | Housing as a % of total capital expenditure |
|--------|------------|-----------------------------------------------|--------|---------------------------------------------|---------|----------------------------------------------|
| 1950 | .. | .. | .. | .. | .. | .. |
| 1957 | 0.4 | 6.9 | 0.1 | 1.7 | 0.5 | 8.6 |
| 1960 | 0.3 | 3.4 | 0.6 | 6.8 | 0.4 | 4.5 |
| 1965 | 0.5 | 4.9 | 1.1 | 10.7 | 0.0 | 0.0 |
| 1970 | 1.2 | 12.6 | 0.6 | 3.8 | 4.1 | 25.9 |
| 1975 | 6.8 | 14.1 | 3.2 | 6.6 | 6.8 | 14.1 |
| 1980 | 18.9 | 13.6 | 25.0 | 3.6 | 13.7 | 9.9 |
| 1985 | 9.3 | 6.4 | 10.8 | 7.4 | 20.8 | 14.2 |
| 1990 | 63.6 | 26.5 | 14.8 | 10.3 | 18.2 | 7.7 |
| 1995 | 16.9 | 12.5 | 7.8 | 5.8 | 18.4 | 13.6 |
| 1998 | 25.1 | 9.8 | 5.8 | 2.3 | 52.9 | 20.6 |

*Sources*:  Estimates of Government's revenue and expenditure; Central Bank of Barbados, annual statistical digests.

## STATUTORY BOARDS AND DEVELOPMENT SPENDING

A substantial part of public investment took place outside of the budget through specialized statutory boards.  In the 1950s and 1960s, several boards were established to assume some of the development functions formerly performed by the central government.  Annual subventions financed upkeep of those that were not self-sufficient.  These boards were managed independently, but were subject to broad official policy guidelines, and financed mainly social services, housing and industry.

**Table 4.3**
**Capital Expenditure by Major Heads: Economic Services, 1950–1998**
**$ million**

| Period | Agriculture | Agriculture as a % of total capital expenditure | Roads and transport | Roads and transport as a % of total capital expenditure |
|--------|-------------|-------------------------------------------------|---------------------|----------------------------------------------------------|
| 1950 | .. | .. | .. | .. |
| 1957 | 0.6 | 10.3 | 3.0 | 51.7 |
| 1960 | 0.3 | 3.4 | 6.5 | 73.9 |
| 1965 | 0.7 | 6.8 | 1.8 | 17.5 |
| 1970 | 1.4 | 8.9 | 3.6 | 22.8 |
| 1975 | 3.6 | 7.5 | 8.7 | 18.0 |
| 1980 | 6.8 | 4.9 | 20.3 | 14.6 |
| 1985 | 19.4 | 13.3 | 30.8 | 21.1 |
| 1990 | 15.0 | 6.2 | 44.4 | 18.4 |
| 1995 | 10.9 | 8.0 | 25.1 | 18.0 |
| 1998 | 17.1 | 6.7 | 81.1 | 31.6 |

*Sources.* Estimates of Government's revenue and expenditure; Government Statistical Service, abstract of statistics; Central Bank of Barbados, annual statistical digests.

The established boards, wholly owned by government and operating off-budget, represented some of the most progressive initiatives of government. Statutory boards such as the Industrial Development Corporation and the Export Development Corporation (these amalgamated in 1992 to form the Barbados Investment and Development Corporation) acted as a forum for educating exporters, providing market intelligence, assisting in marketing efforts, funding joint venture partners and otherwise guiding potential entrepreneurs as they sought to set up new businesses. These institutions performed a tremendous service in preparing the Barbadian business person for the world of trade outside of Barbados during the last 30–35 years of the twentieth century. These services were supported at the level of training by the Barbados Institute of Management and Productivity (BIMAP) to which government made a significant financial contribution.

While some off-budget statutory boards may have failed from a purely financial viewpoint, some offered important externalities in the form of knowledge, technology, greater understanding of the markets and an appreciation of trade and goods. However there were negative externalities as well that may have resulted from government involvement in some activities. For example, the possible creation of a dependency syndrome manifested in a tendency to look to government for solutions to trade and production difficulties.

## CONCLUSION

Government in Barbados, unlike governments in many developed countries, including the Caribbean, was not a major asset holder or a major participant in commercial type activities. Capital expenditure tended to include both the acquisition of assets and major outlays on new services. Barbados did not join the trend popular in the 1960s and 1970s of nationalization of major industries and activities. Consequently, in the era of privatization which was generally being practiced in the developing world and which gave the Latin American capital markets a major fillip in the 1980s and 1990s, Barbados was unable to join on any significant scale, principally because there were few activities to be privatized. Also, in some cases, it proved more useful to ensure profitability before privatization. So that privatization, when it came, was not to save companies or to provide fiscal support to government, as in many developing countries, but to broaden the base of ownership and to deepen the capital markets.

# 5

## Revenue and Tax Structure

**INTRODUCTION**

This chapter examines the objectives of taxation and analyzes the contribution of major taxes to government revenue. Particular attention is paid to the relative role of direct and indirect taxes, more especially their impact on demand, on income distribution and on work incentives. Corporate and personal taxation particularly are evaluated with emphasis on their impact on risk-taking behavior and are compared with the impact of indirect taxes on risk-taking. Special emphasis is placed on the evaluation of policies of "industrialization by invitation," more especially their results for accelerated economic growth and for the encouragement of entrepreneurship.

Two important aspects of tax policy are efficiency and equity. In the search for revenues, the objectives of policy makers are often to minimize the negative effects on economic efficiency, so that social and redistributional objectives may be attained while minimizing disincentive effects.

However, the assumption that markets function in a way that produce pre-tax results of price equal marginal cost is not likely to hold in practice in developing countries (Lewis, 1984). Governments therefore need to initiate actions that will transfer resources. Taxes are a means of transferring resources from households to government or to enterprises. They influence incentives and impact on the decisions of consumers and investors and on the extent to which persons or entities engage in certain types of activity.

Considerations such as how tax on income and assets influence risk-taking behavior, or influence investment decisions and affect profitability are

therefore important. Equally important are concerns about how taxes
influence savings and hence economic growth. There is however, little
literature on which to make comparisons of the impact of growth. Marsden
(1983) employed a sample of 20 countries for the period 1970–1979 to
assess the relationship between taxes and economic growth. He concluded
that there was a negative association between the overall tax-GDP ratio
and economic growth. Most studies instead look at the relationship between
expenditures and economic growth rather than revenues and economic
growth. However, tax incentives are assumed by economists to have an
important impact on promoting economic growth, and most theorists
advance that the structure of taxation can both assist and retard economic
growth.

An equally important concern is how varying economic groups are
influenced by the tax system and how this flows through to investment and
output. Also, uncertainty about the outcome of investment decisions can be
affected by tax changes and changes in relative benefits due to the
particular clauses in tax laws, and can impact on the willingness of
businesses to take risks. Theoretically, therefore, marginal benefits should
be weighted by social marginal utilities of income and the effect of policy
changes in tax revenue should be factored into such measurements.
However, in reality, policy choices are largely determined by evaluations of
likely outcomes based on past responses and likely future responses in the
context of social and economic objectives. The decisions that flow from
such evaluations are likely to be guided by shared objectives but usually
require compromises by several economic groups. This is true of most
systems including the Barbados system.

**OBJECTIVES OF TAXATION**

Government's policy on taxation tended to be aimed at obtaining enough
funds to cover expenditure, at redistributing the tax burden in a more
equitable form and in shaping a tax policy to stimulate economic growth.
Understanding how savings and profits respond to tax changes in a dynamic
model therefore helps us to evaluate the dynamic consequences of tax
changes.

Taxation accounted for over 85% of revenue averaged over the period
1950–1998 (see Table 5.1).

**Table 5.1**
**Summary of Tax Revenues, 1950–1998**
**$ million**

| Period | Tax revenue | Direct taxes | Indirect taxes | Total revenue | Tax to total revenue (%) | Taxes on incomes and profits to total revenue (%) |
|---|---|---|---|---|---|---|
| 1950 | 9.4 | 4.0 | 6.0 | 10.0 | 94.0 | 34.0 |
| 1955 | 14.7 | 6.8 | 8.1 | 16.1 | 91.3 | 38.8 |
| 1960 | 22.5 | 9.7 | 12.8 | 25.2 | 89.3 | 36.2 |
| 1965 | 32.7 | 13.0 | 19.6 | 38.5 | 84.9 | 31.3 |
| 1970 | 75.7 | 37.9 | 38.7 | 87.8 | 86.2 | 37.4 |
| 1975 | 176.3 | 91.4 | 84.8 | 198.5 | 88.7 | 41.7 |
| 1976 | 189.8 | 103.6 | 85.3 | 211.3 | 89.8 | 44.2 |
| 1980 | 387.5 | 186.3 | 201.3 | 441.3 | 87.8 | 36.6 |
| 1985 | 606.5 | 268.3 | 338.1 | 643.7 | 94.2 | 31.7 |
| 1990 | 891.8 | 387.1 | 504.6 | 949.5 | 93.9 | 28.3 |
| 1995 | 1,081.5 | 459.6 | 621.9 | 1,165.8 | 92.8 | 32.3 |
| 1997 | 1,381.2 | 518.8 | 862.2 | 1,458.3 | 94.7 | 29.5 |
| 1998 | 1,464.4 | 565.1 | 899.3 | 1,545.0 | 94.7 | 30.4 |

*Sources*: Estimates of Government's revenue and expenditure; Government Statistical Service, abstract of statistics; Central Bank of Barbados, annual statistical digests.

## The tax system comprised four basic types of tax:

1. Direct taxes on income and profits, that is, company and personal income taxes;
2. Taxes on foreign trade—mainly import duties;

3.  Taxes on goods and services;
4.  Taxes on property—mainly land tax.

Taxes on income and profits formed the major source of government revenue in the earlier period, maximized their share in the mid-1970s and slipped again in the 1990s. During the period 1950–1976 the share of these taxes in total revenue rose from 34% to 44.2%. They represented 6.8% of GDP in 1950 compared with 13.8% in 1976. The yield from these taxes almost doubled during the period, and by 1976 represented 4.17% of total earnings. By 1995 taxes on income and profits represented 32.3% of total revenue and by 1997 had slipped further to 29.5% of total revenue as indirect taxes rose.

It has been argued that generally, public sector pricing and taxation policy suggest that the difference between price and marginal cost is analogous to a tax. However, during the early years of the period under study, taxes were seen as a means of financing expenditures and sometimes as a means of shifting consumption habits.

In many cases the intention of the tax was to produce certain income and substitution effects. These included the intention to encourage switching to low-priced items or to discourage certain types of activities, such as imports of certain goods and services. Often, expenditure switching was influenced by the source of the item and less so its cost, foreign exchange costs rather than domestic costs being the major concern.

## THE RISE OF DIRECT TAXES

During the first 20 years of the period there tended to be a slightly greater dependence on indirect taxes. However, direct taxes predominated in the 1970s and from the 1980s to the end of the century indirect taxes swiftly overtook direct taxes leading to greater dependence on indirect taxes during the latter part of the period. In the early years, Barbados had not yet become the major consuming society which it was later to become. This may explain the dependence on direct taxes in the 1970s. However, compared with developed countries, even when direct taxes were substantial, they did not dominate the budget. In Barbados, direct taxes accounted for 52.4% of total taxes in 1973 compared with 60% in the United States. By 1998, direct taxes accounted for 38.6% of tax revenue largely as a result of the shift in the emphasis to indirect taxes resulting from the introduction of the value added tax.

Direct taxes can also be used as a means of correcting for inequalities in income. Progressive income tax systems are typically evidence of this approach. There was, however, some concern that the incidence of tax was counterproductive and a deterrent to investors and it was revised in the 1990s. It was argued that a highly progressive income tax with rising marginal rates increased the likelihood that risk-taking would be discouraged. This complies with the findings of Peterson (1981) who found that tax rates and economic growth were negatively correlated in developing countries through their effect on savings. Allowable deductions help to offset this, but the presence of allowable deductions for losses is usually "ex post" and are not likely to override disincentive effects.

Peterson's 1981 study also found a positive correlation between indirect taxes and economic growth. Such findings may help to explain the tendency during the 1990s to shift toward lower direct taxes and higher indirect taxes. At the level of indirect taxes, the role of the tax has implications for interpretation of tax elasticities. If the role of an indirect tax is intended to be a deterrent to consumption, then it can be argued that tax revenue is raised most efficiently by taxing goods or factors with inelastic demand or supply. However, where revenue raising is the main objective then government would prefer a tax with a high income elasticity. These factors become important in evaluating the relative emphasis on direct and indirect taxes.

## PERSONAL INCOME TAXES

Personal income taxes made a considerable contribution to total tax revenue by any standard. These taxes rose from 21.3% of total taxes in 1950 to 31.1% in 1976 and fell in the 1980s as levies and other indirect taxes were imposed. By 1997 this ratio was 17% even though by then many levies had been removed. The system of personal income tax was a simple graduated one and the incidence of the tax was progressive. In the period 1950–1957 rates ranged from 3% on incomes of $500 and over to 75% on incomes $24,000 and over. In 1957, 5% was charged on incomes of $1,000 and the maximum rate chargeable remained unchanged at 75%.[1] In 1971 allowances were altered to allow for the separate assessment of the income of husbands and wives earned in the income year 1970 and thereafter. Basic allowances[2] were increased and the maximum rate was lowered from 75% to 65% chargeable on incomes over $30,000. Data for 1962 and 1973 show that the amount of revenue forgone through personal allowances fell on a per capita basis (in current prices) from $1,370 to $1,050. In constant prices the allowances are roughly the same when adjustments are made for inflation, that is, allowances tended to keep up with the cost of living. Real per capita allowances, however, tended to represent a progressively smaller percentage of total income since incomes rose faster than prices. There was an experiment in 1987 with massive tax allowances and lower effective income tax rates but this was quickly reversed. By the early 1990s there was a perception shared by the IMF that personal income taxes and corporate taxes should be integrated and that the form of the taxable entity should not influence the rate of tax. The maximum rate was integrated with the corporate rate at 40% and by the end of the century their importance in total revenues had slipped considerably.

Cash flow problems and delays in collection occurred from time to time. Government was able to alleviate the first problem through the introduction of a pay as you earn (PAYE) system. The PAYE system was first introduced in April 1957 and applied to incomes of persons who were not self-employed. In 1973 incomes of self-employed persons were placed on a partial PAYE basis, and in the same year, companies were required to pay part of their taxes as they were currently earned, that is, on a partial PAYE basis.[3]

A shift toward lower direct taxes was evident in the early 1990s as a stabilization instrument. A traditional argument is that taxes on income play an important role in stabilization. If aggregate income is rising and government taxes away increasing proportions of real income, this has a dampening effect on the expansion of the economy and reduces inflationary pressures. The contrary holds when aggregate income is falling; that is, the reduction in the overall tax burden as income falls stimulates demand and increases inflationary pressures.

Planners never adopted strict indexation, and possibly wisely so, However, accommodation was made for the effect of inflation when wage contracts of government workers were negotiated, but there was no indexation. Wage increases tended to be roughly related to the rate of inflation when prices were rising, and less so when prices were slowing. To this extent, the wages of government workers tended to reduce the stabilization properties of the progressive income tax structure. Generally, where discretionary changes are "ad hoc", the timing of these changes ought to relate to the economic situation. Generally, wage negotiations due at the expiration of contract periods tended to be implemented regardless of whether the economy was in an upswing or downswing and hence tended to be pro-cyclical at times.[4]

Despite their continued rise, personal income tax receipts represented a declining proportion of taxable income. Tax payable fell from 23% of taxable income in 1962 to 18% in 1973 mainly as a result of larger allowances. A major explanatory factor behind the continually favorable collections, despite tax rate reductions, was the high elasticity of the tax with respect to GDP. However, the disincentive effects of high direct taxes led to a series of reviews in the second half of the period and by 1998 personal income taxes were representing only 16% of total revenues.

The personal income tax system was not frequently altered, but each alteration when it did occur, tended to be aimed at influencing income distribution or work incentives. Changes in the tax system did lead to some redistribution. In 1962, 13% of the people reporting to the Inland Revenue Department paid 37.9% of the tax; by 1973, there was evidence of some redistribution, 7% of the people reporting paid 23.3% of the revenue raised from personal income taxes.

Data for the later period were not available. However, during the early period data showed that Government employees tended to contribute substantially to personal income tax receipts. According to the 1970 census, only 17% of the workforce was employed in the government service in that year, but 25% of taxpayers were government employees. Government employees therefore had a higher filing rate with the Inland Revenue Department. In addition, government made significant recoveries on its wage bill and the rate of recoveries increased each year. Almost one-tenth of the wages and salaries of government employees were returned to the Inland Revenue Department by way of income taxes in 1974 compared with one-fifteenth in 1962.

The need for a high sensitivity of tax receipts to income tended at times to run counter to the need to encourage incentives to work and to take risks. The possibility that the joint assessment of husbands' and wives' incomes (which resulted in higher taxes) might have been deterring females from entering the labor force prior to 1970 was an instance of such a clash. Corrective measures were taken in 1970. This illustrated that though a policy on personal income taxes can help to stimulate economic growth by increasing productivity, a tax structure also has the potential for retarding economic growth.

It is often argued that the tax rate has no impact on savings when income is below a minimum level but that only beyond a certain level of income does the tax rate impact on savings and investment. In the later years, the importance of saving was emphasized in the form of tax incentives for investment in shares in venture capital funds and in mutual funds. These tax incentives were quite successful. Mutual funds rose from $6.6 million in 1996 to $112 million at the end of 1999. The inference is that such savings would have been made principally by the higher income groups.

## COMPANY TAXATION

Many adjustments in corporate taxation took place in the first 27 years of the period, that is, 1950–1976. In the early part of the period company receipts were the major revenue earner, between 1950 and 1956 company tax receipts exceeded personal income taxes and between 1956 and 1963 they kept pace with each other. Largely because individual incomes were low. However, from 1964 onward, personal income taxes progressively outpaced company taxes so that by 1976, revenue from this source was twice as great as that originating from companies (see Table 5.2). Several allowances, tax incentives and tax concessions designed to stimulate business investment were responsible for the relative decline in company taxation. The share of company taxes in the total of tax revenue fell consistently during the period, from 24.8% in 1950 to 15.5% in 1976, to 14.6% in 1980 and by 1998 had fallen to 11.1% of total revenue. Company taxes tended to be relatively inelastic. An estimate of overall elasticity shows company tax elasticity averaged 0.8 in the period 1976–1990 (see Table 7.3).

Tax holidays were implemented as part of a wider industrialization drive. However the evasive action taken by that section of the corporate sector which benefitted from these tax arrangements was not taken into account until some time after this policy had been in operation, so that the full benefits of tax receipts were not derived from this measure for most of the period.

Depreciation rules and the treatment of losses also formed an important part of tax policy. These influence the general investment environment and are taken into account by businesses in making decisions relating to types of investment and types of valuation techniques. These aspects of corporate taxation were more explicitly taken into account in tax policies of the 1980s and onward but were not given a great deal of emphasis in the 1950s and 1960s.

**Table 5.2**
**Taxes by Major Categories, 1950–1998**
**$ million**

| Period | Corporate taxes | Personal income taxes | Consumption taxes | Stamp duties | Import duties | VAT |
|---|---|---|---|---|---|---|
| 1950 | 2.4 | 2.9 | - | | 4.4 | - |
| 1955 | 4.5 | 3.0 | - | | 6.1 | - |
| 1960 | 4.6 | 4.6 | - | 0.3 | 8.7 | - |
| 1965 | 5.6 | 6.4 | 1.6 | 0.3 | 11.5 | - |
| 1970 | 13.3 | 16.2 | 4.3 | 0.7 | 21.2 | - |
| 1975 | 30.3 | 44.4 | 9.6 | 15.5 | 31.2 | - |
| 1980 | 64.7 | 89.0 | 51.4 | 5.2 | 89.7 | - |
| 1985 | 56.8 | 134.5 | 99.9 | 74.5 | 96.9 | - |
| 1990 | 95.1 | 139.9 | 197.3 | 101.1 | 117.8 | - |
| 1995 | 133.5 | 213.6 | 308.9 | 90.7 | 93.1 | - |
| 1998 | 171.9 | 268.0 | 0.2 | 14.5 | 136.9 | 455.1 |

*Sources*: Government of Barbados Economic Report; Estimates of Government's revenue and expenditure; Government Statistical Service, abstract of statistics; Central Bank of Barbados, annual statistical digests.

In the 1960s, however, the country was faced with competitive terms from neighboring islands aimed at encouraging industrialization when "industrialization by invitation" was being generally promoted in almost every island in the Caribbean. This was based on the argument that a high company tax rate discouraged the formation of new companies and therefore retarded the growth of enterprise and that easy terms would attract foreign capital. The dilemma that faced government was the desire to increase investment, encourage industrialization and, at the same time, meet expenditures. The inelasticity of company taxes partly illustrates the policy choice made by government. That is, government chose to sacrifice revenue for increased investment by the corporate sector. A second argument in favor of easing company tax rates was that high taxes might frequently be paid out of undistributed profit rather than dividends, and that taxation would not therefore release real resources, but would cut down savings by the private sector. Despite these advantages, the number of companies paying taxes rose by 50% in the 11-year period 1962–1973, and the sector became less dominated by a few large companies. In 1962, 44 companies paid two-thirds of the tax, in 1973, 33 companies paid one-third, suggesting a change in concentration in the industry.

Companies were taxed at the rate of 40% of taxable profit for much of the period. This was eroded to some extent by a number of capital allowances.   Allowances rose 73.6% in the period 1962–1973, and represented 18–21% of taxable profit.   Relief was granted to several struggling companies. This negated part of the tax so that the effective rate of tax averaged 32.7%.

The share of indirect tax declined during the 1970s and rose during the rest of the period. Indirect taxes contributed to 53.0% of revenue in 1950 and 40.4% in 1976 and by 1998 were contributing 58.4% of total revenue. Import duties were still the most important indirect tax despite the slowdown in tax collections. Other taxes include taxes on consumption, land, retail sales, motor vehicles and motor spirits. Excise taxes are one of the oldest taxes in the fiscal system, but revenue from this source was quite small, partly because domestic production of the taxed items has not grown at the same rate as incomes (see Chapter 8 on reform of indirect taxes).

## IMPORT, CUSTOMS (STAMP DUTIES) AS REVENUE AND INCENTIVE TOOLS

Work by Tanzi et. al  (1987) shows that import duties are positively influenced by the openness of the economy and negatively influenced by the level of per capita income and by the country's reliance on domestic taxes on goods and services. This is borne out by the case of Barbados, which became more open during the period under study.

Import duties, stamp duties (stamp duties) were all taxes on imported goods. During the 1970s, the country depended more on exploitation of internal taxes with diminishing relative reliance on taxes on international trade. Therefore, whereas import duties and stamp duties accounted for about two-thirds of indirect taxes in 1950, they accounted for only 55.2%

in 1975 and 47.1% in 1980.[5] By the 1990s taxes such as consumption taxes had overtaken custom duties in importance. The increasing number of exemptions was also partly responsible for the reduction. However, by 1995 customs revenue/stamp duties still accounted for 16% of revenue compared with ratios as low as 1% in some developed countries.

The decline in importance of customs/stamp duties was partly the result of a conscious effort on the part of government to reduce taxes on capital and intermediate imports in an effort to encourage local production and stimulate business initiative, and partly as a result of the imposition of other indirect taxes on luxury items. As a result, the average elasticity of the tax fell during the first half of the period. Since rates charged on luxury items were also raised during the latter period, the lower overall elasticity of the tax in the second half of the period suggests that the loss in taxes from granting allowances on imports of capital and intermediate goods may have outweighed the gains from higher taxes on luxury items.

Between 1950 and 1975 the average ratio of import duties to GDP was 6.3%, that is, for every $100 increase in GDP receipts from imports rose by $6.30. In addition, the tax shows an average overall elasticity of 0.96 when discretionary changes are taken into account, indicating that customs duties increased at a slightly slower rate than GDP. However, tax rate changes affecting customs duties occurred quite frequently. These changes and the exemptions that partially offset them account for the difference between the built-in flexibility of the tax (0.7) and its overall elasticity (0.96). The low overall built-in flexibility of the tax suggests why frequent fiscal measures were needed to maintain the tax take from customs duties (Williams, 1991b).

Between 1955 and 1965 when a range of measures was taken to encourage industrialization (e.g., the Pioneer Industries Act, 1958 and the Industrial Incentives Act 1963), notable changes also took place regarding the role of import duties. In 1963, import duties were abolished on 27 items in an effort to stimulate domestic production. Duty on imported furniture was raised in 1967, duty on fabric lowered and imported garments were made subject to increased taxes in efforts to promote the furniture and garment industries. These measures were directed at influencing the allocation of resources into priority uses and at stimulating domestic production and export in specific areas. By 1995 import duties accounted for 8% of tax revenue. However, by that time several other taxes such as consumption taxes and stamp duties were in place. These were subsequently replaced by the value added tax.

## CONSUMPTION TAXES TO RESTRAIN IMPORTS

Consumption taxes were imposed for the first time in 1962 to stabilize imports. Since most of the taxed items were imported, there was little real distinction between customs duties and consumption taxes. When receipts from consumption taxes are included with import duties, instead of the falling share of customs duties in indirect taxes as noted earlier, taxes on international trade actually rose from 53.0% in 1950 to 56.6% in 1976. However, these taxes really took off in the 1980s when they were heavily used as deterrents to consumer imports. Between 1979/80 and 1980/81 consumption tax receipts more than doubled as the country used this device to stabilize consumer imports. The elasticity of the two taxes taken together was slightly higher but this was a result of frequent increases in consumption tax rates. The taxation of luxury items was an attempt to add a degree of progressivity to the tax system since the higher consumption duties were chargeable mainly on luxury items, but it is doubtful whether the tax was progressive to any appreciable extent.

Generally, the introduction of luxury taxes is based on the assumption that, given the highly unequal distribution of income, and low rates of private sector saving, there exists a substantial surplus in the form of luxury consumption at the upper end of the income scale (Lewis, 1984). Because luxury consumption usually means a heavy import component and because scarce foreign exchange is of vital importance for development, the use of the luxury tax gains additional importance. The use of a luxury tax was very evident during the 1991–92 stabilization program when it was imposed on motor cars and other luxury items in an effort to reduce rising consumerism.

## TAXES ON INTERNATIONAL TRADE AS POLICY TOOLS

Customs duties (and consumption taxes) were used, not only to protect domestic producers, but also to reduce consumption and importation. For example, in 1968 and again in 1977, taxes on luxury items were increased markedly. These impositions were intended to cut back consumption and so increase the savings ratio (S/Y) and thus, the potential rate of capital formation. Such charges also tend to depress inflationary pressures by raising prices relative to factor incomes.

In 1973, customs duties were placed on 376 items in an effort to conform to the CARICOM agreement relating to Common External Tariffs (CET). This did nothing to stimulate domestic production. The imposition of these taxes tended rather to reduce savings and disposable incomes, particularly since they coincided with a recession of 1974–1976, when both national product and importation of goods declined in real terms. The increased tax rates seemed excessive and tended to aggravate the recessionary situation and the already low levels of demand, and made the attainment of a high rate of economic growth more difficult to achieve.

In the years that followed, particularly in 1976 when the balance of payments situation began to worsen, government was faced with the choice of increasing revenue from indirect taxes on imports and a consequent worsening of the balance of payments at the expense of declining revenues. In 1982 significant modifications were made to stamp duties in response to the effort to stabilize imports as part of the stabilization program. However, subsequent modifications were not especially significant until 1992 when major changes occurred (see Chapter 8 on reform on the tax system).

Lewis (1984) shows how tariffs can support the exchange rate. He argues that tariffs are a part of the price of foreign exchange. He notes that they take away purchasing power from users of imports and transfer them to government.

Since tariffs raise the price of some imports they restrict the demand for foreign exchange at the existing exchange rate. By doing so they make possible a lower price of foreign exchange than would otherwise be the case if tariffs were not present and if the same tax revenue were raised by other means. (For example by way of income tax, a sales tax, that applied to both foreign and domestic goods and export tax.)

Tariffs provide a domestic producer of competing goods with higher returns for production on substitution for one dollar of imports than is earned by a producer of exports with one dollar. When the producer is also able to buy his capital goods and his intermediate imports at a lower tariff, he is also able to buy foreign exchange at a lower price (and sell at a higher price). This is in fact a subsidy. Tariffs subsidize both new and old producers unless tariffs rates are lowered over time. Using the argument of Lewis (1984), one would conclude that tariffs helped to support the exchange rate during the 1970s and 1980s until they were reduced in the 1990s.

## OTHER INDIRECT TAXES

Barbados' experience with other indirect taxes such as restaurant sales and retail sales tax was undistinguished. The first was introduced in 1971 and was abandoned only when VAT was introduced in 1997, while the second was short-lived, having been abandoned in 1976 largely because of collection problems. It was introduced in November 1974 and abolished in September 1976. Both taxes were based on the value of goods and services purchased and were therefore flexible and elastic. Taxes imposed on motor vehicles were imposed mostly to conserve foreign exchange and to modify conspicuous consumption behavior. They were partly successful in reducing imports of vehicles when they were linked to specified down payments. In later years when the Hire Purchase and Credit Sale regulations were removed it was personal credit worthiness which tended to be the limiting factor controlling these imports, but in the interim other marketing initiatives contributed to increasing the car import bill before it stabilized toward the end of the century. However, they tended to underperform and to be unresponsive in inflationary conditions. A completely new regime was however, introduced with the introduction of the value added tax, which by the end of the century had become the single most important tax among government's revenue raising measures. The system was both a response to globalization and trade liberalization and also to a recognition that the country's system was in need of a tax overhaul.

## CONCLUSION

Except for the revenue raising objective of taxes on international trade, the objectives related to controlling imports, stimulating of local production and encouraging business activity were fortunately all complementary. However, multiple objectives led to a tendency to make adjustments to various indirect taxes so as to protect certain activities or to achieve one of the many declared objectives. For example, reducing taxes on capital and intermediate goods to encourage investment. During the 1990s the impetus of trade liberalization tended to remove some of these multiple objectives from the indirect tax system, leaving only the tax collection objective and offering no replacement means of encouraging local production. The rate of tax itself was influenced by international trade agreements so that indirectly the tax take itself was similarly influenced, but more importantly, the cost structure of local production was heavily influenced by agreements made at the international level. Compliance with these agencies is proving to be a major challenge at the beginning of the twenty-first century.

The view that sectors which benefit from government expenditures should also contribute to its revenues was a view which prevailed from time to time. For example, that the tourism sector benefits from major infrastructural developments, roads, airports, harbors etc., all of which are costly. It is implied that these activities should be taxed at the point of expenditure (room rate, restaurant or exit tax) so as to recover revenues to maintain the necessary infrastructures for these specific services. While there was an element of this in the tax system, for the most part revenues were pooled and were used to finance any type of expenditure. The tax specific approach was however given prominence in many Latin American countries where, for example, the cost of road building was funded through a road toll or road tax. However, in Barbados, for the most part, proceeds of tax revenue were not tied as to specific uses.

## NOTES

1. Because of the relatively high degree of monetization and the relatively high literacy rate, the country has little problem with defining and assessing taxable income.

2. Taxpayers were given allowances for dependents, for medical expenses, for alimony and covenants.

3. For example, if the public sector wage increases of 1969 and 1973 had been made in the downswing of the cycle they would have tended to be stabilizing.

4. An additional tax on income is the contribution to the National Insurance Scheme. The scheme provides sickness and retirement benefits. This additional tax on incomes does not go directly to the central government but, is nevertheless, part of the total tax effort made by individuals.

5. In 1975 customs duties accounted for only one-third of indirect taxes. In that year, receipts from new taxes—the levy on sugar exports and the retail sales tax, were responsible for most of the increase in the indirect tax rate.

# 6

## Government Revenue and Tax Performance, 1950–1976

### INTRODUCTION

This chapter examines three aspects of taxation—tax capacity, tax performance and taxation as a stabilization tool. Revenue responsiveness and the elasticity of various revenues are also an important part of the analysis. The chapter perceives government as managing the tax system to achieve developmental objectives while ensuring macroeconomic stability. It pays particular attention to the capacity of government to tax and the obligation of government to reduce or increase taxation in line with total output. Finally, it evaluates the role of the tax system in effecting expenditure-switching policies, and assesses the implications of such policies. The period is divided into three phases: phase one—the period 1950–1976 (Chapter 6), phase two—the period 1976–1990 (Chapter 7), and phase three—the 1990s (Chapter 8). The first period saw the use of traditional tax measures applied in an incremental fashion, the second was a period of ad hoc introduction of tax measures, and the third, a period of tax restructuring.

### PHASE I: GOVERNMENT REVENUE AND TAX CAPACITY, 1950–1976

One of the general hypotheses upon which most economists agree is that emergent nations must increasingly mobilize domestic resources at rapid rates if they are to accelerate economic growth, and that public revenues are particularly important in attempting to achieve accelerated economic progress. The tax structure must therefore be able to generate proportionately higher revenues through discretionary action (i.e., tax rate and base changes, legislative action and improvements in techniques of collection) as well as through automatic increases in revenue. Tax rates must be sufficiently high to finance government expenditures, but not high enough to stymie initiative and enterprise.

In Barbados, revenue as a proportion of GDP was fairly stable between 1950 and 1963. In the period 1951–1955 revenue rose very slowly (3.2% per annum) then accelerated in the years 1961–1970 and slowed again in the early 1970s. In the period 1950–1976 revenue rose almost eighteen-fold and GDP twelve-fold. A country's tax ratio (tax/GDP) is an important tool in explaining the changing structure of government revenues and taxation in particular. What the overall tax/GDP ratio shows is the proportion of national income that is compulsorily transferred to the government sector for public purposes. This ratio gives an idea of the division of responsibilities between the public and private sectors and suggests the degree of control that the government can potentially exercise over the disposition of purchasing power in the economy. The tax ratio for Barbados was fairly high. Lotz and Morss (1967) in a comparative study of developing countries cited tax ratios of 5% to 18% and Chelliah et al. (1975), in another cross-country study, cited average tax ratios of 13.6% in 1966–1968 and 15.2% in 1969–1971.[1] The average tax ratio for the period 1969–1971 in Barbados was 26.6% (see Table 6.1).

The pressure for increased revenues to finance GDP elastic demand for social goods and services requires that revenue increases at a faster rate than GDP. A few cross country studies have found perverse results with respect to tax revenue and GNP. Marsden's (1983) empirical work—in which he regressed the real average annual growth rate in the 1970s of each of 20 countries or its corresponding ratio of tax revenue to GDP—found a statistically significant negative relationship between growth rates and tax shares. Similar results were derived from a World Bank study on the subject. This is quite the reverse of the Barbados story.

Generally, economic growth depends not only on revenues but on political stability, education, training, use of technology, quality of the labor force and on several other factors. These must all be taken into account in evaluating the relationship between economic growth and public finances. However, many of the contributing factors are not easily measurable so that they often remain untested mathematically. Other studies (Mancur Olson, 1982) find no reliable connection between the size of government and economic growth. Generally, however, the views of many economists tend to point to agreement that a growing nonmarket sector tends to be associated with a lower rate of economic growth and a larger market sector with a higher rate of growth. Observation of government's share of GDP (see Table 2.1) would suggest a growing non-market sector in the 1970s and 1980s with a slight reduction in the 1990s.

In Barbados, revenue was relatively responsive to GDP during the period 1950–1976.    Revenue responsiveness is measured by the historic responsiveness of the tax source as GDP increases.[2]

$$E = \frac{\% \text{ change in revenue}}{\% \text{ change in GDP}}$$

The overall revenue performance of a revenue structure is enhanced if taxes are elastic.

**Table 6.1**
**Taxes/Revenue/GDP, 1950–1976**

| Period | Revenue/GDP (%) | Marginal rate of taxation (%) | Taxes/GDP (%) |
|--------|-----------------|-------------------------------|---------------|
| 1950   | 20.0            | ..                            | 17.3          |
| 1955   | 16.4            | 40.0                          | 14.3          |
| 1960   | 20.1            | 14.2                          | 17.9          |
| 1965   | 24.3            | 8.5                           | 20.7          |
| 1969   | 29.9            | 54.8                          | 25.1          |
| 1970   | 30.3            | 7.5                           | 26.1          |
| 1971   | 31.4            | 29.5                          | 27.1          |
| 1975   | 28.3            | 50.3                          | 25.2          |
| 1976   | 26.8            | 65.2                          | 24.1          |

*Sources*: Government of Barbados Economic Reports; Estimates of Government's revenue and expenditure; Government Statistical Service, abstract of statistics; Central Bank of Barbados, annual statistical digests.

The average revenue elasticity in Barbados over the 27-year period 1950–76 was significantly more than one, 1.182, and average tax elasticity

1.184. Normally, when tax revenue elasticity is greater than 1, and tax revenue is growing faster than income, government can increase recurrent expenditure in the knowledge that it would be financed by normal tax yield.

However, efforts by government to raise elasticity can adversely affect the incentive to work and to take risks. A high tax-GDP ratio is therefore generally associated with increasing taxpayer resistance and disincentive effects. It is interesting to note that when the tax-GDP ratio was at its highest in 1975 and 1976, the country was exhibiting either low or negative growth rates, that is, the public sector seemed to be exerting fiscal drag on the economy.

The ability to tax is determined largely by the country's taxable capacity and it is possible to consider an almost infinite list of variables that could conceivably affect taxable capacity. Furthermore, imperfections in measuring capacity are unavoidable. In most studies the level of per capita income is taken to reflect the level of "surplus" over subsistence out of which taxes could be paid as well as the level of economic development. Indicators such as the literacy rate, the level of monetization, urbanization and so on, point to the ability of government to collect taxes. However, definitions of subsistence change over time, as can be seen by the changing tax threshold determined by government for individuals filing annual tax returns. Indicators, such as per capita income and the degree of openness, influence the ability of people to pay taxes. A high per capita income generally reflects both a higher level of development, and therefore, a higher capacity to pay taxes.

Hinrichs (1966),[3] in a comparative study of 40 developing and 20 developed countries found that though per capita income is a good indicator of tax capacity in developed countries, in developing countries the degree of openness is a better indicator. In a similar study, Chelliah (1971) uses per capita income, export ratio and the mining share as indicators of taxable capacity. Lotz and Morss (1967) found that both per capita income and openness (as measured by imports plus exports as a percentage of GDP) significantly influenced the tax ratio. They also found it an appropriate measure of taxable surplus.

In Barbados, since the country is highly dependent on sugar exports, and agriculture controlled a significant share of GDP during phase one, 1950–1976, the share of agriculture in GDP has been included as an explanatory force. It is intended also as an indicator of the level of development and is anticipated to be negatively related to the tax ratio.

Per capita income is also used as an indicator of tax capacity. The measure of openness is the Lotz-Morss measure—imports plus exports as a percentage of GDP.[4] This, rather than the pure import ratio of Hinrichs,[5] has been used, in view of the policy of lower tax rates or tax exemptions on intermediate capital goods. Using the above indicators, with data for the period 1950–1976 the equation for taxable capacity was calculated. The share of agriculture in GDP was included because of its importance in the economy during that time and a measure of openness and per capita income were included as well.

The equation for taxable capacity is given by:

$$\hat{\frac{T}{Y}} = 11.97 - 0.081 \, A/Y + 0.012 Y_p + 0.036 \, F/Y$$

$$(1.78) \quad (-0.75) \qquad\quad (1.88) \qquad\quad (1.68)$$

| Period | R2 | D.W. | F ratio |
|--------|------|-------|---------|
| 1950–1976 | 0.69 | 0.883 | 17.27 |

where

$\hat{\dfrac{T}{Y}}$ = taxable capacity

$A/Y$ = the share of agriculture in GDP;
$Y_p$ = per capita income; and
$F/Y$ = Lotz-Morss measure of openness (imports and exports/GDP)

Tax performance can be looked at as the basis of indices of tax effort in the static sense. The following expression for the tax ratio can be used to estimate tax effort (E):

$$T/Y = f(\hat{T/Y}, E)$$

Linearizing and rearranging gives:

$$E = \frac{T/Y}{\hat{T/Y}}$$

where

$$\frac{\hat{T}}{Y} \quad = \quad \text{taxable capacity}$$

T/Y      =   tax ratio

Tax effort is measured by the actual tax ratio over the tax ratio estimated according to taxable capacity.

When this measure is used, taxable capacity was greater than the actual level of taxation particularly in the period 1959–1966 (see Table 6.2). The untaxed capacity meant that tax effort was below average in those years. (When the tax effort is below one, tax effort is low and when above one, tax effort is higher than average.) One of the factors that explains the below average tax effort in the pre-1968 period was the need for streamlining of the tax system. This came in 1968 and resulted in a vast improvement in the tax effort (see Table 6.2).      This means that in the years 1950, 1951, 1957, 1959–1967 and 1973–1974, the amount of taxes could have increased, particularly between 1961 and 1963 when untaxed capacity was at its highest.

Fiscal policy therefore tended to fluctuate between periods when the system underperformed and periods when it overperformed.    In the 1950–1976 period the index of tax effort reached a high of 1.16 in 1976 and a low point of 0.8 in the early 1960s. In the periods when the economy was performing below capacity it tended to be further from the average than in periods when it overperformed.

The additional marginal product that government has been able or thought fit to direct to the public sector is measured by the marginal tax rate, that is, the absolute change in tax revenue over the absolute change in GDP (see Table 6.1).  It measures how fast the tax ratio rises over time.  The marginal rate was quite high in Barbados but was fairly stable until 1975 and 1976, when it rose to 50.3% and 65.2%, respectively. The average for the period 1950–1976 was 31%.  This tends to corroborate the evidence of a continually increasing tax ratio (see Table 6.1).

It may be argued that a higher per capita income indicates a greater taxable surplus and therefore a potentially larger tax base.  A positive correlation between $Y_p$ and T/Y tends to give credence to this hypothesis.

**Table 6.2**

**Measures of Tax Capacity and Tax Effort, 1950–1976**

| Period | Estimated tax capacity (%) | Index of tax effort | Potential for increase in tax effort (%) (+ above average) |
|---|---|---|---|
| 1950 | 17.9 | 0.974 | 2.7+ |
| 1951 | 19.8 | 0.999 | 8.7+ |
| 1952 | 17.9 | 1.011 | 1.1 |
| 1953 | 16.9 | 1.104 | 9.4 |
| 1955 | 17.5 | 1.147 | 0.1 |
| 1956 | 18.6 | 1.023 | 0.0 |
| 1957 | 19.1 | 0.907 | 10.2+ |
| 1958 | 19.0 | 1.116 | 10.4 |
| 1959 | 19.0 | 1.004 | 0.4+ |
| 1960 | 19.4 | 0.926 | 8.0+ |
| 1961 | 20.3 | 0.859 | 20.7+ |
| 1962 | 20.4 | 0.841 | 18.9+ |
| 1963 | 20.8 | 0.838 | 19.3+ |
| 1964 | 21.6 | 0.98 | 2.0+ |
| 1965 | 21.6 | 0.948 | 5.5+ |
| 1966 | 21.7 | 0.964 | 3.7+ |
| 1967 | 22.1 | 0.965 | 3.6+ |
| 1968 | 22.3 | 1.041 | 3.9 |
| 1969 | 23.5 | 1.117 | 10.1 |
| 1970 | 23.9 | 1.204 | 2.3 |
| 1971 | 25.8 | 1.033 | 3.2 |
| 1973 | 25.9 | 0.978 | 2.3+ |
| 1974 | 25.7 | 0.922 | 8.5+ |
| 1975 | 24.2 | 1.111 | 10.0 |
| 1976 | 24.1 | 1.164 | 14.1 |

The correlation coefficient between these two variables was 0.8. However, the size of the taxable surplus and the possibility of increasing the tax ratio does not in itself imply that tax rates should be increased. Decisions to increase taxation should depend upon judgments about the benefits from using resources in the private sector compared with the benefits obtained from use by the government sector in the form of expenditure on goods and services. The equation was tested separately for the period 1964–1976 and the results were as follows:

$$T/Y = 43.36 - 0.427A/Y - 0.006Y_p - 0.56 F/Y$$
$$\quad\quad (2.97) \quad (-0.025) \quad (-0.74) \quad\quad (-0.621)$$

(The t-statistics of the coefficients are in parentheses.)

Results

| $R^2$ | D.W | F ratio |
|-------|------|---------|
| 0.73  | 1.68 | 8.20    |

## CONCLUSION

Generally, the country's taxable capacity rose consistently during the first 25 years of the period under study. Tax effort was generally stable except for the 1960s when there was considerable scope for increases in tax effort (see Table 6.2).

### NOTES

1. No adjustment has been made for differences in fiscal systems.

2. The measure of elasticity used throughout the study includes revenue resulting from discretionary measures and is referred to as elasticity. Revenue resulting from only normal growth in income will be referred to as the built-in flexibility.

3. The raison d'etre of Hinrichs' hypothesis is that the degree of openness (imports as a percentage of GNP) provides, directly and indirectly, easy tax handling. In Barbados one-third of revenue came from import duties. This was partly a result of the openness of the economy and imports were therefore easy to tax.

4. Bahl (1971) includes the size of the foreign trade sector, the agricultural share and the mining share of GDP.

5. Hinrichs' measure of openness does not indicate a reduction in the level of openness as would have been expected in view of efforts to restrict imports. The Lotz-Morss measure did indicate such a reduction.

# 7

---

# Tax Performance, 1976–1990

## INTRODUCTION

The performance of the tax system in the period 1976–1990 was particularly instructive. During this period the system was constantly subjected to short-term modifications and tax adjustments that were intended to be temporary, but many of which lasted several years. The introduction of special levies in the period 1982–1992 was particularly indicative of the need for a tax overhaul. This chapter uses an empirical approach to the evaluation of tax policy and specific taxes during the period 1976–1990. The data series was cleaned of discretionary changes in order to evaluate the impact of particular taxes. An econometric analysis of the period was used to evaluate the income elasticity of these taxes in order to assess responsiveness to changes in output.

## PHASE II: TAX POLICY AND TAX CAPACITY, 1976–1990

Compared to the years 1950–1976, changes in the tax system in the 1976–1990 period were quite dramatic, particularly in the 1980s. There was a shift from the incremental approach used in the previous years to one of major changes in tax rates, often simultaneously in several areas. This put tremendous stress on the system and on the predictability of policy outcomes. This section examines the performance of tax policy over that 15-year period,[1] 1976–1990, and seeks explanations of causes leading to tax rate and base changes during the period, both in terms of conventional approach of expenditure needs and the ability to tax and in terms of wider macroeconomic considerations.

Government's control over the disposition of purchasing power is measured here by the tax ratio, that is, the proportion of national income that is transferred to government. This rose gradually throughout the period, accelerated somewhat in 1988 and 1989 to almost one-third of the national product, fell in 1990 but remained high at 29.7% compared to 25.2% a decade earlier (see Table 7.2). This gradual increase in the tax ratio was, however, deceptive since it was supported by rapid changes in tax rates.

## RELATIVE TAX RATIOS

Barbados' tax ratio was high relative to some Caribbean countries and compared quite favorably with others at the beginning of the 1980s. This position changed dramatically toward the end of the decade. The table below shows that while the tax burden in 1987 amounted to 27.4% of GDP in Barbados, in Trinidad and Tobago it was only slightly lower at 26% (down from considerably higher levels at the beginning of the period) but was twice that of Jamaica where the rate had declined from 27% at the beginning of the 1980s to 13% in 1987. Indeed the trend of an increasing tax ratio in Barbados during the period is in direct contrast to the trend observed in these other two countries. A comparison of tax/GDP ratios for Trinidad, Jamaica and Barbados are as follows:

|      | Trinidad | Jamaica | Barbados |
|------|----------|---------|----------|
| 1980 | 36       | 27      | 25.2     |
| 1985 | 30       | 12      | 27.8     |
| 1987 | 26       | 13      | 27.4     |

Cross-country analysis of this kind must, however, be cautiously interpreted since the level of services provided by government and therefore the claims on disposable incomes differ dramatically across countries. This affects the net economic cost of the tax to the taxpayer and the true tax burden. However, the contrasting trends are instructive.

## TAX OBJECTIVES

The main assumption behind most analyses of government expenditure is that government's primary reason for imposing taxes in order to reduce disposable incomes is to protect the balance of payments. Secondly, taxable capacity must first exist, and a policy of reducing disposable incomes is rarely planned and is often forced on governments. Thirdly, taxing in order to reduce disposable incomes in one period to transfer taxable surplus to a later period with the intention of reducing the need to increase taxes in later periods, usually encourages governments to spend those receipts on new services, thus making the new level of government expenditure a more permanent part of the recurrent budget.

## TAX CAPACITY, 1976–1990

The major constraint on government's ability to meet expenditures through taxation is the country's taxable capacity or the ability to impose taxes without creating disincentive effects or reducing output. The conventional literature relates this to the size of the tax base and the major contributors to output, as well as to imports, or imports plus exports. Personal incomes and company profits, proxied by per capita GDP and the combination of major sectors to GDP, are often included among these determinants.

The presumption here is that the limit of taxable capacity is reached when additional taxes lead to lower output, that is, when taxes exert a fiscal drag on the economy. This is an important sign to government that taxes and consequently expenditures must be reduced. Because of the difficulty in reversing government expenditures without major policy shifts, it is therefore often precautionary for government to keep the tax ratio below tax capacity, that is, to ensure that its tax effort is comfortably below one (see Table 7.2).

The following section attempts to examine the tax implications of these assumptions in the Barbados context during the 1980s. An attempt was made to determine taxable capacity using several combinations of the variables referred to earlier. The most acceptable results were achieved using per capita GDP, imports and the share of tourism in GDP. The final regression results are given in Table 7.1.

The t-statistic for per capita GDP was rather low and its standard error rather high, but this did not seem sufficient to abandon the equation. The high standard error is possibly explained by increases in the tax base and income distribution considerations. Results are based on 14 observations—1976–1990.

Table 7.1

**LS Regression Results:  Dependent Variable Is T/Y**

| Variable | Coefficient | Standard error | T-stat | 2-tail sig |
|---|---|---|---|---|
| Constant | 0.240667 | 0.047199 | 5.0989749 | 0.003 |
| Per capita  GDP | 2.3921465 | 2.1117303 | 1.1327898 | 0.281 |
| Imports | -0.1119404 | 0.054567 | -2.0514023 | 0.065 |
| Tourism | 0.7165402 | 0.3637566 | 1.9698342 | 0.075 |
| | | | | |
| R-squared | 0.747422 | Mean of dependent var | 0.0270393 | |
| Adjusted R-squared | 0.678537 | SD of dependent var | 0.022652 | |
| S.E. of regression | 0.012843 | Sum of squared residual 0.85031 | 0.02652 | |
| Durbin-Watson stat | 1.87098 | F-statistic | 10.85031 | |
| Log Likelihood | 46.3696 | | | |

The results of the above equation were used to calculate tax capacity ratios.  These were shown to be slightly higher than the actual tax ratio for the periods under consideration, indicating that the tax effort was below capacity for all of the 1980s (see Table 7.2).  In the series used, tax effort (i.e., the ratio of tax ratio to the tax capacity) was only above capacity in one year—1978.  While the results of the equation may be reasonably reliable with regard to the direction of tax effort, that is, in judging whether tax effort is increasing or decreasing, the results may be imprecise in indicating the absolute levels of tax capacity and tax effort.  This is because the actual coefficient turned out by the analysis will vary slightly with the choice of variables entered into the equations.  The use of the more reliable trend analysis of tax capacity and tax effort indicates that other than 1978, tax effort fluctuated mildly during the decade reaching its peaks in 1983, 1985 and 1989.  The critical question is whether the size of the margin below tax capacity is sufficient to stave off disincentive effects and fiscal drag. It is interesting to note that three years of negative growth in the 1980s, that is, 1981, 1982 and 1990, while not themselves years of the highest tax effort, were years preceded by two years of relatively high tax effort (see Table 7.2). In view of the negative growth in 1990 it does, however, tend to suggest that high government expenditures in precipitating the need for higher revenues were likely to exert fiscal drag on the economy in 1991 if further taxes were raised.

The fact of a 75% $R^2$ in the least squares regression and the knowledge that not only fiscal considerations but the need for balance of payments correction also led governments to increase taxes, prompted the search for a fuller explanation of the tax ratio that included these considerations. While the approach used earlier (a modification of (Chelliah, 1971; Hinrichs, 1965; Lotz and Morss, 1967) explains the capacity to tax, it does not explain the influence on the tax ratio of other macroeconomic variables.

A least squares regression equation that included the fiscal deficit, GDP per capita and foreign exchange reserves lagged one period, came closer to filling this vacuum. The estimated equation was:

$$T/Y = 215.4 - 0.29R + 0.64 \text{ Def.} + 91085 \text{ Yp} + 311.4 \text{ Im}$$
$$(-1.54) \quad (3.0) \qquad (11.0) \qquad (-1.8)$$

$$R^2 = 0.98 \qquad \text{D.W.} = 1.11$$

The equation yielded a high $R^2$ of 0.98. Not surprisingly, there was a high level of serial correlation. The DW was 1.11. However, the results reinforced the view that there was a high correction. While this confirms this relationship, further study of this aspect of the tax ratio would be useful in order to integrate this aspect quantitatively into the analysis in a manner that aids decision-making.

It is, however, suggested that the tax approach to correcting a deficit on the balance of payments works only if these receipts are frozen. Where they are used to finance increased government expenditures in the form of additional services, the tax becomes permanent in nature or an equivalent tax may be sought as new expenditures become an entrenched part of the recurrent budget.

## MARGINAL TAX RATES AND BUOYANCY

Over the period 1976–1990 the average tax buoyancy was 1.14, that is, government raised proportionately more taxes relative to increases in nominal output (see Table 7.2).

**Table 7.2**

**Selected Tax Indicators, 1976–1990**

| Year | Tax capacity | Index of tax effort | Revenue/ GDP | Taxes/ GDP | Marginal rate of taxation | Tax buoyancy index |
|------|------|------|------|------|------|------|
| 1976 | 25.1 | 0.96 | 26.8 | 24.1 | .. | .. |
| 1977 | 26.0 | 0.95 | 27.7 | 24.6 | 28.2 | 1.15 |
| 1978 | 25.5 | 1.04 | 31.2 | 27.6 | 56.3 | 2.04 |
| 1979 | 27.3 | 0.97 | 29.6 | 26.6 | 22.0 | 0.83 |
| 1980 | 27.5 | 0.92 | 28.7 | 25.2 | 20.4 | 0.81 |
| 1981 | 27.4 | 0.89 | 27.5 | 24.4 | 16.7 | 0.69 |
| 1982 | 27.2 | 0.95 | 27.7 | 25.8 | 57.2 | 2.21 |
| 1983 | 27.5 | 0.96 | 28.5 | 26.4 | 36.1 | 1.36 |
| 1984 | 28.5 | 0.91 | 27.6 | 25.8 | 19.5 | 0.77 |
| 1985 | 29.1 | 0.96 | 29.5 | 27.8 | 66.2 | 2.38 |
| 1986 | 31.1 | 0.89 | 29.2 | 27.7 | 26.6 | 0.96 |
| 1987 | 31.7 | 0.86 | 29.1 | 27.4 | 23.4 | 0.84 |
| 1988 | 32.3 | 0.95 | 33.1 | 30.7 | 79.5 | 2.59 |
| 1989 | 32.3 | 0.98 | 34.1 | 31.6 | 42.4 | 1.33 |
| 1990 | 32.2 | 0.92 | 31.9 | 29.7 | 50.0 | -1.68 |

*Note:* GDP data are on a calendar year basis: taxes and revenue data are on a fiscal year basis.

This was primarily because of major discretionary changes in tax rates and the tax base. In 1982,[2] 1985 and 1988 the marginal rate of tax exceeded 50% (by increasing amounts on each occasion and thereafter declined only to be increased again three years later to a higher nominal tax rate delivering a higher tax buoyancy coefficient (see Table 7.2). A rachet effect is therefore observed in the pattern of marginal tax rate and tax buoyancy suggesting that it was predictable that the year 1991 would witness some major increases in taxes in the absence of significant expenditure reductions or efficiencies. (Basic consumption taxes were raised from 10% to 12%.)

It is noteworthy that the major contributors to this buoyancy of the tax rate and to an overall marginal rate of taxation—31% for the period—were stamp duties and levies followed by consumption taxes and corporation taxes (mostly a result of surcharges).[3]


## TAX ELASTICITY AND BUILT-IN FLEXIBILITY OF THE TAX

While the basic reason for resorting to major discretionary tax changes in this almost predictable fashion lay in an unsustainably high level of expenditures relative to tax revenues, a microanalysis of individual taxes shows that several of these taxes were inelastic with respect to output (when discretionary changes are excluded) and even more inelastic with respect to the tax base (see Table 7.3). This explains the need for frequent changes in the tax rate and the tax base in the 1980s and would have been an important argument for the introduction of the value added tax in 1996.

Conventional income (GDP) elasticity analysis was applied to the major taxes (see Table 7.3). This showed that personal income taxes and company taxes had income elasticity coefficients (including discretionary changes) very close to the built-in flexibility of the tax, (i.e., calculated after cleaning the series of discretionary changes).

Indications are that levies, consumption taxes and stamp duties carried high income elasticity coefficients; levies, possibly because they are not subject to any deductions and adjustments, carried a high built-in flexibility and consumption taxes a slightly higher built-in flexibility (i.e., after discretionary changes are removed from the series). Since consumption taxes tend to be used as an instrument to deter importation of certain goods, this result was not surprising.

Import duties showed both low income elasticity and a low built-in flexibility with respect to income (see Table 7.4). The analysis indicated that direct taxes had greater built-in flexibility with respect to income than indirect taxes and were therefore able to sustain their growth without resorting to frequent tax base changes—up to 1986.

**Table 7.3**

**The Response of Tax Revenue to GDP, 1976–1990**

**(Results of single equation ordinary least squares regression)**

|  | Ratio | $R^2$ | Elasticity coefficient |
|---|---|---|---|
| Tax ratio | 25.2 |  |  |
| Marginal tax rate | 31.7 |  |  |
| Income elasticity of personal incomes taxes |  | 0.31 | 0.39 |
| Income elasticity of company taxes |  | 0.82 | 0.8 |
| Income elasticity of levies |  |  | 2.9 |
| Income elasticity of direct taxes |  | 0.83 | 0.8 |
| Income elasticity of indirect taxes |  | 0.99 | 0.8 |
| Income elasticity of import duties |  | 0.92 | 0.8 |
| Income elasticity of stamp duties |  | 0.91 | 3.48 |
| Income elasticity of total taxes |  | 0.98 | 2.2 |
| Income elasticity of total taxes |  | 0.98 | 1.14 |
| Income elasticity of total revenue |  | 0.98 | 1.09 |

## SHIFT FROM DIRECT TO INDIRECT TAXES, 1976–1990

In analyzing the share of direct and indirect taxes in total tax receipts it is observed that the year 1984 was a watershed in the traditional share of direct taxes in total tax receipts. During the decade there was a marked switch from direct to indirect taxes particularly during the period 1984–1987 when the share of indirect taxes rose from approximately half of total taxes in 1983 to as high as almost two-thirds in 1986—in just three years. This share remained high for most of the 1990s. Because direct taxes pre-1986 (particularly personal income taxes and levies) tended to grow continually in line with output and were sticky downward, they provided an anticyclical buffer not found in indirect taxes, particularly in the pre-1986 period. It is, however, quite appropriate for a tax system to have a combination of taxes that respond—some procyclically and others anticyclically—to GDP changes. Since governments traditionally do not restrict expenditures as national output falls, some tax instruments must be available on which government can depend in periods of low growth. At the same time, however, taxes which are procyclical afford consumers the choice of adjusting expenditures where income is declining.

However, since there is rarely a downside flexibility in government expenditures the share of direct and indirect taxes in total tax revenue should be split so as to provide a more appropriate balance. While it is possible that the increased personal allowances, concessionary adjustments in tax bands and reductions in the maximum marginal tax rates in 1981–1984 may have been appropriate to reduce fiscal drag in years of negative or low real growth, the acceleration of this trend in years of positive growth coupled with major switches to indirect taxation seem to have introduced instability and unreliability in tax receipts.

## TAX CONCESSIONS AND PERSONAL INCOME TAXES, 1976–1990

Elasticities of individual taxes were calculated using log linear regression—both with respect to income and with respect to the tax base (see Table 7.4). A closer examination of individual tax performance revealed some interesting statistics. Income elasticity of personal income taxes including discretionary changes was calculated at 0.8 (pre-1986). This is a slightly inelastic coefficient. The series was cleaned of discretionary changes in order to calculate the built-in flexibility of personal income taxes. The built-in flexibility of the tax turned out to be 0.8. This is partly explained by the large negative changes largely offsetting the years of large positive changes and by increasing wages during the period. The experience confirms that personal income tax receipts tend to be sticky downward in the presence of declining real GDP. In years of negative growth, 1981 and 1982, personal income taxes grew by an average of 10% per annum despite concessionary adjustments in the tax bands and increased personal allowances. In the year 1983, a year of no appreciable growth and a year in which the maximum marginal rate of tax was reduced from 70% to 60%, personal income tax receipts continued to rise. In 1986 however, the massive concessions in personal income taxes far outstripped the ability of the elasticity of these taxes to offset such a change, leading to a reduction in personal income tax receipts of $72.7 million over the two-year period 1985 and 1987. This pushed the elasticity coefficient of the tax to 0.4 (see Table 7.4). In addition, these concessions took place against a background of low wage settlements—the wage index rose 5.1 and 2.4 percentage points during that period in contrast to 1983, when personal income tax concessions were made against a background of higher wage settlements (the index rose by 11.6 percentage points in 1983). This would have increased the tax base despite almost zero growth in that year.

**Table 7.4**
**Elasticities and Built-in Flexibility of Various Taxes, 1978–1998**

|  | Income elasticity includes discretionary changes | Built-in flexibility with respect to income | Elasticity with respect to tax base | Built-in flexibility with respect to tax base |
|---|---|---|---|---|
| Personal income taxes | 0.4 | 0.8 | .. | .. |
| Company taxes | 0.8 | 0.8 | .. | .. |
| Levies | 2.9 | 1.0 | .. | .. |
| Consumption taxes | 2.2 | 1.2 | 2.5 | 0.7 |
| Import duties | 0.8 | 0.5 | 0.9 | 0.5 |
| Stamp duties | 3.5 | .. | 3.79 | .. |

The tendency of personal income tax receipts to grow consistently from year to year was partly explained by increases in wages that are often in excess of output increases. This partly accounts for the only slight inelasticity of the tax up to mid-1980s. In the absence of data on taxable income, it is suggested that the tax base elasticity of personal income taxes is possibly higher than its income elasticity. It also suggests that the built-in flexibility of the tax with respect to the tax base (i.e., tax base elasticity calculated after cleaning the series of discretionary changes) is still quite positive and tends to confirm that the tax tended to be anticyclical. It is unclear however, whether this anticyclical aspect of the tax was evident in the pre-1986 period.

## NATIONAL OUTPUT AND COMPANY TAXES, 1976–1990

The performance of corporate tax receipts tended to mirror output performance sometimes with a slight lag and seemed to respond more to growth in real output than to growth in nominal output. For example, company taxes performed very badly in 1984 and 1985 following years of negative growth of 1981 and 1982 and zero growth in 1983, declining in absolute terms in 1983 and 1984, despite a 3% surcharge on corporate profits. The share of income and profits in total taxes in also declined sharply in 1986 and 1987 (see Table 7.5). Similarly, the 15% decline in corporate tax receipts in 1990 may well have been directly related to the 3.3% decline in real output in 1990.

This seems to suggest that pure-revenue earning considerations are not the best basis for changes in the rate of corporate taxation. The 3% surcharge in corporate profits imposed between 1982 and 1984 actually coincided with a decline in corporate profits related to financial difficulties being experienced by marginal firms in a recessionary situation. This was evidenced by increases in bankruptcies and receiverships during the period. It is suggested that the 1983 surcharge was ill-timed.

The 1988 surcharge on corporate incomes was imposed in a more conducive economic environment when corporate tax receipts were much more buoyant. (Revenues from corporate taxes rose 29.5% in 1988.) Available data revealed that corporate taxation was only slightly inelastic with respect to output, having an income elasticity coefficient of 0.8 inclusive of discretionary changes in the tax base and the tax rate. This suggests that as GDP increased company tax receipts increased slightly less than proportionately. The presence of tax concessions to the manufacturing sector, and various loss carry forward provisions, prevent a transparent relationship between corporate profits and tax receipts in any one year. However, the pressure of concessions mainly served to confirm the slightly inelastic nature of the tax. (Data were not available on the corporation tax base, i.e., taxable corporate profits.)

Table 7.5

**Share of Income and Profits and Indirect Taxes in Total Taxes, 1976–1990**

| Period | Share of income and profit taxes in total taxes (%) | Share of indirect taxes in total taxes (%) | Total levies $M |
|--------|-----------------------------------------------------|-------------------------------------------|------------------|
| 1976 | 49.2 | 44.9 | - |
| 1977 | 48.5 | 46.3 | - |
| 1978 | 48.8 | 44.1 | 6.1 |
| 1979 | 43.9 | 49.2 | 4.1 |
| 1980 | 41.7 | 51.9 | 3.1 |
| 1981 | 42.6 | 51.4 | -2.7 |
| 1982 | 42.1 | 47.2 | 23.8 |
| 1983 | 38.8 | 50.6 | 25.4 |
| 1984 | 35.2 | 53.9 | 30.1 |
| 1985 | 33.0 | 55.7 | 29.5 |
| 1986 | 25.2 | 61.3 | 43.8 |
| 1987 | 19.8 | 64.7 | 69.8 |
| 1988 | 27.8 | 57.2 | 75.1 |
| 1989 | 26.9 | 58.4 | 86.0 |
| 1990 | 28.0 | 56.6 | 91.3 |

*Source*: Government of Barbados Economic Report; Central Bank of Barbados, annual statistical digests.

## THE RISE OF LEVIES—SUPPLEMENTARY REVENUES

Levies, first introduced in 1978 and relatively unimportant until 1981, played a pivotal role as a revenue-raising measure during 1981 and 1982 when declining output slowed the growth of indirect tax receipts leading to lower tax buoyancy. Levies, ostensibly earmarked for specific expenditures, and at first kept outside of central government revenues, were subsequently placed in the Consolidated Fund as they became a critical part of government revenues. The incidence of the levies was increased approximately every other year since 1981 until 1993. Like personal income taxes, they were more income elastic, were resistant to weakening output over short periods and were a fairly reliable source of revenue.

A calculation of the income elasticity of levies in the 1990s revealed that levies were one of the more income elastic of the direct taxes. The income elasticity of this tax fluctuated wildly during the period examined largely because of the frequent discretionary changes. The average elasticity coefficient of this tax was significantly high, 2.9 (see Table 7.4). It was very difficult to clean the series in order to calculate the built-in flexibility of the tax with respect to income, since rate changes were so frequent. However, based on the remaining years of no discretionary changes, an average elasticity coefficient of 1.1 was calculated showing that the built-in flexibility of this tax is rather high—largely because there were no exemptions, allowances or exclusions compared to other direct taxes. In many ways the performance parallels on the indirect side, the growth of stamp duties both in the timing of its implementation and in its contribution to tax receipts.

In estimating the impact of the tax, there is also a problem of shifting behavior in reaction to the tax. Economic agents can shift taxes on to the workers so that the employer's portion of payroll taxes may well be assumed by the workers. However, it is difficult to confirm the extent to which this takes place.

## INDIRECT TAXES, 1976–1990

### Import Duties: Revenue Unresponsiveness & Caricom Obligations

This category of indirect taxes still contributed significantly to government revenues despite its falling victim to reductions brought about by obligations to the CARICOM trading arrangement. Income elasticity of import duties was slightly low, at 0.8, inclusive of discretionary changes in the tax. When the elasticity of import duties with respect to imports at current prices was calculated, the elasticity of the tax was slightly higher, at 0.9 (see Table 7.4). In addition, trends occurred that were not explained by the data. Data indicate very awkward results with regard to the elasticity of tax receipts collected at the port. For example, in 1984 imports rose by 6.1% and duties fell by 5.6%. Conversely, imports declined and duties increased in

1985–1988 without any evidence of significant changes in the tax base during these years. This may have been attributable to changes in the composition of imports, since different rates of duty apply to different categories of goods. This occurred during a period of dramatic changes in imports of raw material into the electronic subsector most of which would have been duty free and may have been compounded by problems of collection at the port of entry.

### Consumption Tax, 1976–1990—A Continuing Policy Tool

Consumption tax was used more as a policy tool than any other indirect tax instrument imposed at the port of entry. It had the advantage of being used to target specific activities for preferential treatment, for example, to encourage manufacturing activity through the use of exemptions and to discourage consumption of luxury items through the imposition of prohibitively high tax rates. The income elasticity of consumption taxes was high, averaging 2.2. However, the elasticity with respect to the tax base (i.e., imports) was higher, at 2.5 (see Table 7.4). When the series was cleaned for discretionary changes, the tax showed a built-in flexibility with respect to imports of 0.7. Since this tax tended to be used as a policy tool, the higher the rate on specific items, particularly luxury items, the lower imports ought to be. This explains the low elasticity with regard to the import base and the low built-in flexibility of the tax with respect to imports. Exemptions to manufacturers on raw material imports also reduced consumption tax receipts. The relatively high elasticity with regard to income compared to the slightly higher elasticity with regard to the import base, however, suggests that as income increased consumers bought luxury items despite the high consumption taxes.

### PROPERTY TAXES, 1976–1990: PROPERTY AS A DISINCENTIVE TO INVESTMENT: CAN TAXES HELP?

Property taxes are a special kind of tax—a tax on assets—and are not directly related to GDP. A desirable economic system of which the tax system is a part should encourage owners of fixed assets to use these assets to earn income in the knowledge that income earned will be greater than would be earned by selling the asset and investing the proceeds in government securities, though not so high as to dissuade the investor from switching his activity to the officially preferred activities in the productive sectors.

While this approach may address the policy on income earned from fixed assets, it does not address the question of the economic costs of abnormal capital gains on fixed assets. It has been suggested that significant capital gains that can be earned by the sale of assets acts as a disincentive for the investor to invest in officially preferred activities in the productive sector. Investors were able to make sufficient gains on real estate without putting any other factors of production to work. In Barbados, investment in real estate was seen as low-risk, since real estate values were sticky downward.

This situation reduced basically to the question of what could be done to encourage investors to switch to preferred activities without unduly penalizing existing activities. The given response to the problem of direct and indirect taxes was the same, that is, that the perceived profitability of these activities must be enhanced in order to encourage such a switch. An attempt to penalize certain activities in order to encourage a switch to others may entail such large penalties as to discourage any activity at all. Unless the potential profitability of officially preferred activities can be simultaneously enhanced, a policy of penalizing nonpreferred activities must be approached very cautiously. Taxation is only one tool that can be used in enhancing their profitability and is probably best used in concert with others.

## SUMMARY AND IMPLICATIONS

The tax system was generally successful as an instrument of social development. The expressed objective behind the tax concessions of 1981–1983 and 1986 was ostensibly to encourage investment through adjustment of disposable incomes. The evidence suggests that increasing disposable incomes was not enough. The budget of 1989 seemed to have applied the tax credit approach to shares in private companies as a means of stimulating investment. However, it is not clear whether statistically its effect was meaningful.

Tax systems that try to put in place expenditure-switching policies tend to be more difficult to devise. The experience of Barbados with exemptions offered to manufacturing is a case in point. The record shows that taxes simply to raise revenues or to prevent spending are much easier to devise while a tax system designed to effect a switch to investment must be based on much wider considerations of which the tax is only one. Studies have been done on this problem, as it affects the manufacturing sector, but there is not a great deal of consensus on the recommended approach.

As a revenue raising tool the tax system was used somewhat erratically in the 1980s. The experience in this period emphasized the need to avoid ad hoc tax changes in the approach to developing effective tax systems. Where reductions are being considered in those taxes with a built-in flexibility with respect to the tax base or where increases are being considered in taxes that are sensitive to changes in real output, caution is required. Consideration must be paid to the trends in taxable base, that is, wages and corporate profits in order to adequately assess the short- and medium-term implications of these taxes. While reductions in direct taxes are useful to guard against fiscal drag and disincentive effects, a high level of dependence on indirect taxes which have a low built-in flexibility with respect to the tax base will not provide medium-term reliability of tax receipts. Unless the tax is broad-based, increasingly higher indirect tax rates, can themselves lead to lower proportionate receipts and possibly to collection problems.

Government's resort to frequent discretionary changes in the 1980s emphasized that the level of government expenditure needed to be reduced if government was not to be forced to resort once again to frequent discretionary changes in the tax rate. It also seemed appropriate that the share of direct taxes in total taxes be reviewed even though the built-in flexibility and anticyclical nature of this tax had been eroded since it still provided a more reliable source of revenues. However, the tax system had been used somewhat erratically in these years. Indeed, the experience of the 1980s emphasized both the merits and demerits of gradualism in the approach to tax changes.

During the period the level of public awareness of the connection between added services and taxation may not have been appreciated. Normally, if taxes are raised, the public will generally be disposed to restrict their demands for government-initiated services if there is a perception that additional services carry a tax cost. This awareness seemed more evident in the 1990s than in the 1970s and 1980s.

In many ways the incidence of corporate surcharges and levies was evidence of a reluctance to give permanence to increased tax rates and may have been based on a view that an upturn in the economy and higher incomes and output would eventually pull the country out of periods of underperforming revenues, and that the need for temporary measures would therefore be short lived. Frequent discretionary changes were really an indication of the need for a tax overhaul.

## NOTES

1. While the analysis for the most part covers a 10-year period, a 15-year series starting in 1976 has been used in order to provide sufficient degrees of freedom for regression analysis.

2. In 1982 a 3% temporary surcharge on corporate profits was imposed and an across-the-board stamp duties of 2%.

3. In 1985 stamp duties were increased from 3% to 12% and consumption taxes raised as well. In 1988 a 5% surcharge on personal incomes and a 7.5% surcharge on corporate profits were introduced.

# 8

## Tax Reform in Barbados in the 1990s

### INTRODUCTION

This chapter discusses structural changes in the tax system in the 1990s following several ad hoc initiatives in prior years. It emphasizes the introduction of the value added tax (VAT), and analyzes the implications of the VAT for revenue collection for inflation and for business incentives. It also places specific emphasis on the commitment to a common external tariff in the region and its implications for the tax system generally, for government revenues and for the competitiveness of manufacturing output.

### PHASE III: FUNDAMENTAL TAX CHANGES

The 1990s witnessed fundamental changes in the tax and revenue systems. Arising out of the structural adjustment program of 1991–1992, government was committed to revising both the direct and indirect tax systems. Most of the revisions were, however, postponed until after the country had completed its 18-month term under the IMF stabilization program.

Tax reform, when it came, was aimed at simplifying the tax system, removing biases in the tax structure, ensuring that the system was equitable and that it took account of differences in income levels and of the implications for disposable incomes. Government implemented the project for direct tax reform in 1992 and postponed the more complex and controversial issue of indirect tax reform until 1997.

In the case of direct tax reforms, in 1992 two rates were introduced for individuals, a 25% minimum rate of tax and a maximum tax rate on individuals of 40% effective from January 1, 1993. Most allowances were removed in an effort to reduce tax avoidance. The exemption for pension income was also withdrawn and substituted with a lower tax. This tended to affect mostly higher income earning pensioners. The stabilization tax and most levies were removed in an effort to simplify the tax system.

In the case of corporations, the stabilization tax was also eliminated. The issue was the integration of the tax rates, that is, whether there should be an absolute corporation tax independent of the individual income tax, or whether the two forms of taxation should be integrated with corporation source earnings taxed at the shareholder level only. The decision to reduce the number of tax bands was accompanied by the removal of most deductions in order to simplify the tax. The overall corporate tax rate was raised to 40%. The change was intended to relieve companies of some costs and permit them to increase employment by easing their cash flow. The overall impact on corporations was positive since the increased costs from the higher corporate rate was substantially less than the saving from the abolition of the stabilization tax.

While most of the tax changes in 1992 were direct tax changes, there was one significant tax change. That was the change in the structure of the land taxes and increases in the rate of tax. Taxes on residential land with owner-occupied dwellings were charged a 0.35% rate on the first $100,000 while the general rate was 0.95% of improved value. This gave some ease to the small property owner. Agricultural land was allowed a 50% discount.

## THE COMMON EXTERNAL TARIFF

During the period, the reduction in the rate of the common external tariff (CET) also influenced revenues and the operational costs of businesses. The CET was introduced in 1973 as a result of a decision taken by CARICOM governments to protect the region from excessive competition while putting in place some noncompetitive means of achieving this objective. The CET operated over the intervening 18 years until 1991, when another decision was taken by CARICOM governments to lower the tariff. This was viewed with some apprehension by several sectors in the region. However, in the midst of a tide of pressure for trade liberalization, the Caribbean had little choice but to lower the CET. Rates were lowered from a range of 0% to 65% to rates ranging from 0% to 35%.

Mascoll and Harding (1992) show that for the Barbados case, the 30% and 45% rates were responsible for 76.5% of the actual revenue collected.

They further observed that textiles and leather subsectors were expected to experience a dramatic fall in protection (from 35.1% to 19.4%) as a result of a maximum CET rate of 20%. A rate of 35% implied a fall in protection of 9.6%. They also found that the effect of raising the minimum CET from 0% to 5% was not significant for the overall economy. They noted that neither the direction nor the magnitude of the effects were easy to determine and that an increase in the tariff did not guarantee more revenue and, conversely, lowering the tariff did not imply less revenue. Whether the change in tariff on the goods had an adverse effect on revenue depended on the elasticity of demand for non-CARICOM goods in Barbados. They noted that while in the short-run the pattern of trade was not likely to change, in the medium to long-run lower rates on extra-regional goods could result in less demand for CARICOM goods. However, governments might opt to impose higher import duties if demand switched from CARICOM to non-CARICOM goods. Overall they concluded that though raising the maximum rate would raise the cost of living slightly (0.7%), this would be more than offset by the lowering of maximum rates to 45%, 35% and 20%, so that the general outcome should be a decline in the cost of living.

## VALUE ADDED TAX

Barbados introduced the value added tax (VAT) on January 1, 1997. Its introduction was the outcome of several discussions with financial institutions, more especially the IMF during the period of structural adjustment in 1991–1992. VAT is a general retail sales tax with a series of credits from taxes paid at each earlier stage of processing and distribution. The most common form of the VAT is the "destination principle." Using this system, sales destined for the domestic market are taxable regardless of their origin (importation or domestic production) and sales "destined abroad" or to export markets are exempt. According to the destination principle the tax burden is alleged to lie in the consuming of a good and it has no protective side effects. Value added taxes have increased in popularity since the early 1960s and have become an acceptable device for harmonizing tax structures among countries in an economic community or customs union.

The objective of the introduction of the VAT was to simplify the indirect tax system, ensure equity in the tax structure and reduce the cascading effect previously evident in the indirect tax system. The VAT replaced principally consumption tax and stamp duty but in addition there were over 14 different types of tax that were in effect, having been imposed from time to time by different administrations in efforts to raise revenue. Studies by consultants commissioned to study the subject argued that existing taxes distorted the tax system and introduced unnecessary complications in production and consumption decisions and were subject to cascading effects.

Normally, if a manufacturer's level tax is truly a single-stage tax, then transactions of intermediate goods among manufacturers should be exempt from taxation, otherwise the tax will cascade just as a turnover tax does, that is, the tax will be included in every other level of transaction thereafter.

The VAT became effective from January 1, 1997. It replaced 11 taxes, mainly consumption tax and stamp duty as well as surcharges, some of which had contributed to the cascading effect of the tax system. An excise tax was imposed on petroleum products, tobacco, alcohol and motor cars and the VAT rate was imposed on the excise. The VAT was intended to be revenue neutral, but the first year of VAT receipts suggested that receipts exceeded expectations by a substantial sum.

Most VAT systems include zero rated or exempted items. In the Barbados case the approach was to minimize the number of zero rated and exempted items. It was originally intended that there should be two rates of tax—0% rate and a 15% rate. However, representations made by the tourism sector that exempt status would result in substantial costs to the industry resulted in the introduction of a third rate of 7.5% for the tourism sector.

The regulations called for a 7.5% rate for accommodation in hotels, inns, guest houses and so on, and the standard rate of 15% for other vatable supplies that are not zero rated. Also, after the first 18 months of operation the VAT was again reviewed and in late 1998 a number of food items were exempted from the VAT. Persons whose supplies of goods and services exceeded $60,000 were required to register and to pay VAT. VAT was made payable on output, but registrants could claim a credit against tax payable on inputs. Several services such as financial services, real estate, transportation, medical and dental services were given exempt status, that is, such supplies were not subject to VAT. However, a person who made exempt supplies was not entitled to claim allowable input tax to recover the VAT paid or payable on goods and services used in making exempt supplies. Other services were zero rated. (Zero rating differs from exemption in that, while in neither case is VAT payable on sales a zero rated sale attracts credit for VAT paid on inputs to that sale. Zero rating is the only way that an activity can be completely relieved of VAT) (Bristow, 1993).

## THE IMPACT OF VAT ON REVENUE COLLECTIONS AND ON INFLATION

The initial impact of VAT was to raise substantially more revenue than was originally intended. VAT receipts for the first full year exceeded receipts from the taxes it replaced (consumption tax and stamp duties). There was no refund of taxes for items imported and taxed but not sold, so that during the early stages of implementation, there was a tendency for imports to be held to a minimum so as to reduce the tax paid at higher pre-VAT rates. By mid-year, however, much of this adjustment had been made.

While the introduction of VAT resulted in lower tax rates on some items, it also imposed higher rates on a wide-ranging number of items and was applicable to both goods and services (unless exempted). The result was that prices rose by 7.7% in the year of implementation of the VAT, but by 1998 inflation rates had returned to pre-VAT levels of around 3%.

Eighteen months after the implementation of VAT, an evaluation was made of its impact that led to relief being given to lower-income groups in the form of an exemption from VAT on a number of basic items.

## CONCLUSION

The introduction of the VAT was relatively smooth, though several post-VAT adjustments were made to the system. VAT entailed the introduction of extensive administrative machinery and substantial record-keeping both by the private and the public sectors. However, receipts from this source exceeded expectations and even after adjustment for VAT relief to the lower income groups, continued to be a significantly improved source of revenue.

# 9

---

# Evaluating Budget Impact

## INTRODUCTION

The effect of the fiscal position on the economy and the impact of economic performance on fiscal choices are discussed in this chapter. Measures of cyclical adequacy are used to determine when fiscal stance should be contractionary or expansionary and how measures of fiscal neutrality can assist in determining the kind of budget that is appropriate under differing circumstances.

This chapter also looks at macroeconomic management and the role of fiscal policy in setting targets and in modifying behavior to achieve preset goals. It argues that the need for modification of fiscal measures in order to achieve certain targets such as output, credit, money supply and balance and payments equilibrium are important to economic stability. While the impact of the budget on the balance of payments is arguably the single most important constraint on the achievement of macroeconomic stability for small open economies, some factors are controllable and others are outside the control of authorities.

The record therefore shows that the extent to which governments can promote economic growth is influenced strongly by the type of fiscal measures chosen but that other constraints can influence governments' ability to efficiently expand the economy.

## IDENTIFYING EXPANSIONARY AND CONTRACTIONARY BUDGETS, 1950–1976

The measure used in this paper to assess the impact of the fiscal position is based on the notion of cyclical adequacy (Dernberg, 1975). The expenditure side is assumed to be neutral if expenditure increases from year to year at the rate of growth of potential output.[1]  A neutral year was selected, 1970, when price stability and balance of payments equilibrium were approximately realized.  Since Barbados suffers from chronic unemployment and since unemployment data are based on sample surveys, no effort was made to select a year of "full employment." However, a year when GDP rose moderately well was selected on the assumption that in such a year, employment would have been average.

This measure of fiscal impact indicates that government maintained a contractionary stance in 16 out of the 27 years (see Table 9.1) varying its stance more rapidly in the last 10 years.  The years of major change in fiscal impact were 1951, 1958, 1969, 1973, 1974 and 1976.  The impact of the budget in these years exceeded the annual average rate of change in GDP—5.0% in constant prices and 10.0% in current prices.  A brief look at these years of major change helps to explain budget impacts.[2]

In 1951, for example the fiscal stance was contractionary.  The private sector was expanding, exports were high and a good sugar crop had led to a 28.3% rise in sugar export receipts and a 17.0% rise in GDP.  There was no need for an expansionary fiscal policy.  Tax receipts rose faster than income and government turned out a surplus.  This led to a contractionary fiscal stance, thus complementing that in the private sector.

The second year of a sharp change in fiscal stance was 1958.  In that year the budget was expansionary.  Activity in the private sector was low. Sugar export receipts fell 26.3% as the sugar crop failed and total domestic exports declined by 21%.  Government therefore engaged in pump-priming of the economy and spending rose phenomenally—38.5% in current prices. In that year the construction of the Deep Water Harbor commenced, a project which accounted for most of the increased spending.

In 1968, despite a deficit government's fiscal stance was contractionary. The low level of expenditure was in response to low revenue yields, particularly from personal income taxes which fell 46.7%.  Expansionary elements in other sectors were mild, and GDP rose by only 6.0%.  In that year, a year following the devaluation of the pound sterling and of the Barbados dollar (at the time the East Caribbean dollar) which was tied to the pound sterling, sugar export receipts fell, largely because Barbados sugar was shipped to the United Kingdom and sugar prices were denominated in sterling.  This had a dampening effect on the economy.  At the same time new consumption taxes were imposed on luxury items and responsibility for the trade tax was taken over by the central government.

**Table 9.1**
**A Measure of Budget Impact, 1950–1976**

| | 1950 | 1951 | 1952 | 1953 | 1954 | 1955 | 1956 | 1957 | 1958 | 1959 | 1960 | 1961 | 1962 |
|---|---|---|---|---|---|---|---|---|---|---|---|---|---|
| *TOTAL EXPENDITURE | 18.9 | 18.2 | 16.3 | 17.3 | 16.4 | 21.5 | 27.2 | 28.9 | 39.0 | 36.0 | 36.4 | 37.9 | 39.0 |
| *REVENUE | 18.4 | 19.5 | 18.0 | 18.3 | 19.7 | 21.0 | 22.9 | 24.2 | 27.2 | 26.1 | 28.9 | 28.7 | 30.4 |
| *REVENUE ADJUSTED | 27.9 | 28.9 | 26.5 | 25.9 | 26.2 | 27.1 | 30.5 | 36.3 | 33.8 | 35.3 | 40.1 | 42.8 | 42.8 |
| *OVERALL DEFICIT | -0.5 | 1.3 | 1.7 | 1.0 | 3.3 | 0.5 | -4.3 | -4.7 | -11.8 | -7.1 | -7.5 | -9.2 | -8.6 |
| GDP | 92.1 | 95.2 | 87.6 | 85.7 | 86.3 | 89.4 | 100.7 | 120.5 | 111.4 | 116.4 | 132.4 | 141.1 | 141.3 |
| TREND EXPENDITURE | 12.0 | 16.1 | 15.7 | 16.1 | 16.5 | 17.8 | 22.3 | 30.5 | 27.4 | 29.6 | 36.0 | 39.7 | 40.7 |
| CYCLICALLY NEUTRAL BALANCE | 15.9 | 12.7 | 10.8 | 9.8 | 9.7 | 9.3 | 8.2 | 5.8 | 6.4 | 5.7 | 4.1 | 3.1 | 2.1 |
| OVERALL BALANCE AS % OF GDP | 0.5 | 1.4 | 1.9 | 1.2 | 3.8 | 0.6 | -4.3 | -3.9 | -10.6 | -6.1 | -5.7 | -6.5 | -6.1 |
| CYCLICALLY NEUTRAL BALANCE AS % OF GDP | 17.2 | 13.3 | 12.3 | 11.4 | 11.2 | 10.4 | 8.1 | 4.8 | 5.7 | 4.9 | 3.1 | 2.2 | 1.5 |
| CYCLICAL EFFECT OF THE BUDGET | 17.7 | 11.9 | 10.4 | 10.2 | 7.4 | 9.8 | 12.4 | 8.7 | 16.3 | 11.0 | 8.8 | 8.7 | 7.6 |
| CHANGE IN FISCAL STANCE: EXPANSIONARY (+) CONTRACTIONARY (-) | | -5.8 | -1.5 | -0.2 | -2.8 | 2.4 | 2.6 | -3.7 | 7.6 | -6.3 | -3.8 | -0.1 | -1.1 |

*These data are in constant 1975 prices

**Table 9.1 (continued)**

| | 1963 | 1964 | 1965 | 1966 | 1967 | 1968 | 1969 | 1970 | 1971 | 1972 | 1973 | 1974 | 1975 | 1976 |
|---|---|---|---|---|---|---|---|---|---|---|---|---|---|---|
| *TOTAL EXPENDITURE | 40.9 | 41.4 | 44.0 | 51.9 | 52.1 | 52.4 | 65.9 | 77.2 | 79.6 | 77.6 | 93.6 | 80.8 | 76.8 | 86.4 |
| *REVENUE | 34.6 | 38.3 | 39.4 | 42.1 | 45.5 | 54.5 | 61.7 | 68.6 | 73.4 | 69.1 | 68.2 | 65.8 | 66.6 | 66.1 |
| *REVENUE ADJUSTED | 49.8 | 48.3 | 48.3 | 50.5 | 54.5 | 58.8 | 59.6 | 68.6 | 70.2 | 69.6 | 70.3 | 72.3 | 66.2 | 66.2 |
| *OVERALL DEFICIT | -6.6 | -2.3 | -4.6 | -9.8 | -6.6 | 2.1 | -4.2 | -8.6 | -6.2 | -8.5 | -25.4 | -15.0 | -10.2 | -20.3 |
| *GDP | 164.4 | 156.3 | 161.1 | 166.7 | 180.0 | 193.5 | 196.6 | 226.5 | 231.6 | 230.4 | 232.2 | 238.5 | 221.1 | 211.4 |
| TREND EXPENDITURE | 48.2 | 46.3 | 48.6 | 51 | 56.9 | 63.0 | 65.1 | 77.6 | 80.6 | 81.1 | 83.2 | 87.5 | 81.8 | 28.3 |
| CYCLICALLY NEUTRAL BALANCE | 1.6 | 1.0 | 0.2 | 4.2 | -2.4 | -4.4 | -5.5 | -7.0 | -10.4 | -11.5 | -12.9 | -15.2 | -15.6 | -12.1 |
| OVERALL BALANCE AS % OF GDP | -4.0 | -1.5 | -2.9 | -5.8 | -3.7 | 1.1 | -3.7 | -3.8 | -2.7 | -3.7 | -10.9 | -6.3 | -4.6 | -9.6 |
| CYCLICALLY NEUTRAL BALANCE AS % OF GDP | 1.0 | 0.6 | 0.1 | 0.0 | -1.3 | -2.3 | -1.9 | -3.1 | -4.5 | -5.0 | -5.6 | -6.4 | -7.1 | -5.7 |
| CYCLICAL EFFECT OF THE BUDGET | 5.0 | 2.1 | 3.0 | 5.9 | 2.4 | -3.4 | 1.8 | 0.7 | -1.8 | -1.3 | 5.3 | -0.1 | -2.5 | 3.9 |
| CHANGE OF FISCAL STANCE: EXPANSIONARY (+) CONTRACTIONARY (-) | -2.6 | -2.9 | 0.9 | 2.9 | -3.5 | -5.8 | 5.2 | -1.1 | -2.5 | 0.5 | 6.6 | -5.4 | -2.4 | 6.4 |

*These data are in constant 1965 prices.

These large increases in revenue were reinforced by constraints on expenditure, so narrowing the deficit. Spending rose only 7.3% in current prices, but an upsurge in the rate of inflation more than offset this increase.[3] Government therefore turned out a surplus for the first time in 13 years and the budget was contractionary. This nevertheless complemented the performance of the private sector where activity had slowed only slightly despite growing inflation and poor sugar earnings.

The expansionary budget of 1969 was a result of several forces. Against a background of poor export performance (sugar exports fell 21.6%), and a relatively small rise in GDP (8.6%) government engaged in pump-priming of the economy.

Spending spiraled, increasing by over one-third, as outlays on health and social services rose. Government workers obtained sizable increases, and though the tax take was fairly high (land tax was taken over from the interim local government in that year) these receipts could not offset the high level of spending. The deficit was $5.0 million or 2% of GDP.

The year 1973 was another significant year. Output was high; GDP rose 18% in current prices and sugar exports were favorable, increasing 17.2%. Despite a high level of output in the private sector, the budget was the most expansionary since 1969. Spending rose 37.5%. The most expansionary element in the budget was substantial increases in the salaries of government workers. Revenues were less buoyant than in 1968 when the budget had also been expansionary. The rates of inflation pushed spending up as prices rose 18.5% during that year. Government's budget tended to feed the inflation. With prices rising and government borrowing increasing, interest rates shot up. The balance of payments registered a deficit of $24.5 million and the budget, a deficit of $42.3 million. This marked the beginning of a trend of relatively large fiscal deficits.

The fiscal stance of 1974 was contractionary (see Table 9.1). Sugar earnings were up phenomenally because of the high sugar prices on the British and world markets.[4] GDP rose over 50% in current prices, but world recession, and price rises of 31.9% offset most real gains. The balance of payments was heading for a substantial deficit. Government contracted its spending sharply and raised emergency revenues in an effort to effect a contractionary stance.

Revenue measures were implemented through rescheduling of company tax payments. The existing system under which taxes were retroactive one year was terminated and a partial PAYE system was introduced. This led to an increase in company tax receipts of nearly 100%. In that year a 5%

charge on retail sales was introduced, water rates were raised and increased consumption taxes were imposed on 27 items. These revenue-raising measures, and the cutbacks in spending led to a decidedly contractionary budget, but activity in the private sector kept growth above trend. The balance of payments registered only a small deficit of $0.4 million.

The depression that occurred in the metropolitan countries in 1974 affected the Barbadian economy in 1975 and 1976. The rate of public spending was high in 1976 only because of a 25% increase in the salaries of government workers; but this was not enough to produce an expansionary fiscal stance since activity in the other sectors was depressed. Exports were down 20% and sugar receipts declined 49.3%, GDP rose only 3.2%. Government deficit rose phenomenally, to $61.6 million in current prices (and $20.3 million in 1965 prices). The economy was under strain to finance this spending since it was just coming out of a year of even deeper depression (when GDP had fallen 7.3%). The balance of payments therefore turned out a deficit of $37.8 million, the largest on record up to that time.

## FISCAL IMPACT ANALYSIS, 1950–1976: STABILIZATION TECHNIQUES

Fiscal management can have adverse implications for macroeconomic management where budgets are either overly expansionary or contractionary at inappropriate times. However, fiscal stance, that is, whether the fiscal accounts have been expansionary or contractionary is not always clear. Methodologies have therefore been developed to test cases that are not clearly expansionary or contractionary so as to assist in determining the true impact of the fiscal accounts.

While the state of the economy affects the budget and the budget affects the fiscal position, it is the economy and not the fiscal outturn which is ultimately more important. Furthermore, the extent of economic growth is not the only determinant of the impact of the fiscal position. Where the size of the desired adjustment does not require major changes in structure and where fine tuning of the fiscal accounts and changes in fiscal stances are effective, then stabilization and fiscal impact adjustments alone are sufficient for stability. This was the case for the period 1950–1976. However, from time to time during the post-1980 period, more radical changes in structure and policies were required. Such periods, of structural adjustment required multidimensional approaches.

A study of the period 1950–1975 shows, that in the years 1957, 1963 and 1970, increases in national product were at their highest (see Table 9.1) yet the budget was contractionary. In 1963 it was expansionary and in 1970 it was virtually neutral.

## DEFICIT FINANCING AND STABILIZATION POLICIES, 1950–1976

The foregoing examination of the years when the budget had a major impact on the economy demonstrates that the capacity of government to accommodate its fiscal stance to that of the rest of the economy depends to a large extent on the size and the direction of the change in national product. For example, if income increases sharply, then it may be appropriate for government to avoid overstimulating the economy (i.e., to aim for a contractionary budget) but this may not be feasible, given the structure of the budget and government's expenditure and revenue commitments. Stabilization thus assumes that government has reserves on which it can draw, that is, that it need not depend solely on revenue, that economic slumps will not persist, and that should Government use its reserves, it will be able to rebuild them.

Barbados tends to suffer short-term embarrassments resulting from fluctuations in the sugar crop and from vagaries in the investment climate both at home and abroad. Theoretically, government ought to run a deficit when there is a short-term downswing in activity. However, the factors that militate against this type of accommodative policy are (1) that expenditure commitments of a continuing nature do not permit cyclical increases and decreases in revenue and (2) that expenditure increases are better confined to the capital budget. However, the lack of cooperant factors also prevents immediate responses.

Lags in responses prevent quick fiscal action. Normally, there is a recognition lag before government perceives how the economy is trending, and an implementation lag (particularly where requests for foreign funds have to be processed). The recognition lag can also be quite long, since policies take time before the impact on the economy is felt. This means that an expansionary budget can consequently occur at a time when it is no longer desirable.

It may be publicly desirable to aim for expansion of the economy at all times but this kind of fiscal stance is not always in the interest of macroeconomic stabilization. Indeed, expansionary fiscal stances can even restrict growth if they produce inflationary and balance of payments problems. Within the 10-year period (1966–1976) the fiscal position was frequently modified  since cyclical fluctuations in the economy became sharper and occurred more frequently.  Government was therefore forced to accommodate its fiscal stance to existing economic conditions.

## FISCAL OUTTURN AND ECONOMIC GROWTH, 1950–1976

Data suggest that the relationship between the deficit and economic growth is only mildly significant, and that deficits need not necessarily lead to higher economic growth nor vice versa.  A regression of GDP per capita on the overall deficit shows a coefficient of determination of 0.68.

The years in which the growth of the economy was above trend were mainly between 1965 and 1971; however, 1956, 1957, 1960 and 1963 were also years of average growth.  These years were, not however, years of the largest deficits.  It is remarkable that the years of large deficits, 1973–1976, were in some cases years of negative real growth, for example, 1975 and 1976.  However, it is not possible to conclude that increasing deficits led to reductions in the rate of growth, since in several of the years of expansionary budgets and moderate deficits, economic growth was above trend. For example, 1956, 1965, 1966 and 1969 (see Table 9.1).  A possible conclusion is that if budgets are excessively expansionary (for example those of 1973 and 1976) they become counterproductive, and far from increasing economic growth may impede the rate of growth if deficits curtail the potential expansion of other poles of growth.

In examining the type of fiscal policies that contributed to the expansionary policies of 1965, 1966 and 1969 (also years when growth was above trend) it is noticeable that during this time several measures were passed to encourage investment—measures which led to reductions in revenues.  In 1964 import duties on 27 items were abolished in order to stimulate local production of manufactured goods.  In 1965 concessions were offered to favor international businesses trading locally.  In 1966 an initial investment allowance of up to 20% for basic industry was introduced. This measure allowed these industries to recover taxed profits up to 120% of the cost of any plant and  machinery.  These expansionary policies, because they were biased in favor of investment, had a positive effect in promoting economic growth in the second half of the 1960s.

A review of the type of budgets and their effects suggests that expansionary budgets achieved through reduction of taxes tended to be more successful than similar budgets effected through increases in spending. The case of the year 1970 tends to substantiate this hypothesis. In 1970 government increased basic personal allowances and allowed married persons to opt for a separate assessment of incomes, thus reducing their tax liability. This measure tended to increase disposable incomes, and had important implications for perceptions about the financial independence of females.

In the same way that financing requirements can inhibit government's potential for expanding the economy, the need to raise revenue can also have the same effect. This can necessitate higher taxes that restrict the rate of growth of private sector savings and investment. This was the case with the rescheduling of company taxes in 1975. Since the inflationary situation of 1975 was already discouraging capital formation, that is, people were spending rather than saving, the additional outlay required from the investing public which almost doubled their tax liability in that year, further discouraged capital formation. This tax measure therefore had serious implications for capital formation and resource allocation. It illustrates that the type of measure introduced is as important as the choice of fiscal stance.

The continuing low and negative rates of growth that persisted despite the expansionary budgets of 1973 and 1976 suggest that whereas the choice of measure, the size of the deficit and the type of cyclical fluctuations influence the capacity of government to stabilize the economy, government can do little to promote growth in a secular slump. Pump priming may increase employment but does not necessarily promote economic growth. This is largely because the budget is often structured for spending on infrastructural projects, and for the development of social and welfare services. In the long run, however, spending can only be supported by a sustained level of economic growth. Prolonged periods of savings and investment seem to have promoted economic growth while economic slumps often mean that services can only be maintained at the expense of further reductions in real growth.

## DETERMINING FISCAL STANCE

During the period 1950–1976, the fiscal deficit was not generated by government dissaving,[5] but by capital account expenditure. Government held to a basically Keynesian stance, increasing expenditures to achieve policy goals. The current account was kept in surplus and a policy of balanced budgeting was pursued. The surplus on the current account was used toward the financing of capital expenditure. Government failed to achieve current account surpluses in only four out of 27 years, 1961, 1963, 1973 and 1976. Between 1950 and 1955, government's overall position was virtually always in surplus and in the period up to 1965 deficits that occurred were generally met by fairly substantial revenue balances built up from surpluses in earlier years. In the post-1972 period, government's deficits spiraled, rising from $14.8 million in 1972 to $61.6 million in 1976 (see Table 9.2).

Between 1950 and 1960, 50% of the current account surplus was transferred annually to the general revenue balance and the other 50%, along with the Colonial Development and Welfare (CDW) grant, were used to finance either social services or were spent on physical infrastructures. The general revenue balance as it was called, was a type of stabilization fund from which capital spending could be met in years when revenue was sluggish.     Grants to the Barbados government under the Colonial Development and Welfare Program (CDW) grew steadily but slowly between 1950 and 1965 from $0.2 million in 1951 to about $1.2 million in 1962 and fluctuated slightly as surpluses or deficits were recorded on government account and as the need for such grants changed. In the mid-1960s, the share of these loans in total expenditure declined as the island moved toward self-government and finally independence. They continued for a few years after independence and finally ceased in 1973. In that year, they met only a small percentage of expenditure. In later periods fiscal deficits were to a greater extent occasioned by dissaving as defined earlier, but still more so by capital expenditures. The size of current account deficits relative to total revenues rose. The most significant case of this was in 1990 when the deficit reached as high as $248 million or 8.4% of GDP (see Table 9.2.)

Local borrowing was increasingly used from the start of the 1960s and was mostly in the form of long-term debentures raised in the domestic market (debenture issues were mostly in maturities of 15–20 years and were issued at low rates of interest). Recourse to foreign borrowing came later. The first foreign borrowing was made in 1957, in the form of a small loan of $0.7 million for the improvement of water resources. Between 1959 and 1966 three large foreign loans were floated on the United Kingdom market totaling $25.7 million in three tranches; $12.4 million in 1959, $6.1 million in 1962 and $7.2 million in 1965. They financed the construction and expansion of the Deep Water Harbor.

**Table 9.2**
**Overall Deficit/Total Debt/Change in Debt Outstanding, 1950–1998**

| Period | Overall deficit ($ million) | Deficit as a % of GDP | Change in outstanding debt ($ million) |
|--------|------------------|----------------|---------------------|
| 1950 | 0.5 | .. | .. |
| 1955 | -0.9 | 0.9 | 1.5 |
| 1960 | -5.2 | 4.1 | 1.6 |
| 1965 | -4.2 | 2.7 | 8.1 |
| 1970 | -11.7 | 4.0 | 8.0 |
| 1975 | -21.6 | 3.1 | 23.1 |
| 1980 | -89.7 | 5.8 | 66.9 |
| 1985 | -125.5 | 6.0 | 140.2 |
| 1990 | -248.2 | 8.4 | 162.3 |
| 1995 | -28.7 | 0.9 | 12.3 |
| 1998 | -51.4 | 1.4 | 75.5 |

*Sources:* Government of Barbados Economic Reports; Central Bank of Barbados, annual statistical digests.

Up to 1965 there was no short-term domestic borrowing. The first issue of three- month treasury bills was made in 1966. The post-1966 period saw several changes in the pattern of financing and in the structure of national debt. In addition to treasury bills redeemable in 90 days, a more active issue of local debentures commenced. Additional funds became available from government, statutory boards, such as the National Insurance Board and the Barbados Savings Bank. They became the major holders of government debt. Also, in 1970 life insurance companies were required to hold a proportion of their portfolio in government debentures. This marked the beginning of government compulsory lending schemes.

In the post-1972 period compulsory lending schemes were further developed. In 1973, commercial banks were required to hold a specified percentage of their deposit liabilities in government securities.[6] This meant that the government held a captive market in government securities. The

Central Bank assumed the traditional role of banker to the government in 1973 and stood ready to provide short-term advances. This added a new dimension to government financing. It meant that a money-financed deficit was possible.[7]

On the foreign markets, funds were obtained in increasing amounts from financial development institutions such as the Canadian International Development Agency (CIDA) and the Inter-American Development Bank (IADB) for specific development projects.

## FISCAL OUTTURN AND ECONOMIC GROWTH, 1976–1998

In the period 1976–1998 there was no observable direct relationship between the fiscal outturn and economic growth. Some very important changes in per capita income took place between 1976 and 1980—these were the years of fastest growth in real terms—yet only two of these years were years of significantly large deficit/GDP ratios. Similarly, between 1981 and 1987 (excluding 1983) when the deficit/GDP ratio exceeded 5%, the per capita growth rate, except for 1986, did not exceed 3.5%. Similarly, between 1994 and 1997 growth rates averaged 3.5% but deficit/GDP ratios were under 2.5%. The story may not therefore be in the fiscal outturn itself, but in the composition of revenues and expenditures and in polices to promote economic growth and to transform the economy. The years 1977, 1984 and 1989, years of the most significant fiscal deficits to GDP (in excess of 8%) were years of average or negative growth, 3.6%, 2.4% and -3.3%. A regression of fiscal deficit on real GDP reveals no relationship during this period and is possibly explained by the increasing complexity and diversification of the economy, as compared with the earlier period 1950–1976, when the relationship was relatively stronger, a time at which the economy was less diversified and the public sector played a more significant role in the outturn for economic growth.

## FISCAL POLICY AND CROWDING OUT

The extent to which government can promote economic growth is constrained by its financing requirements. These can sometimes crowd out the private sector and retard economic growth. In 1973 it can be argued that government's expansionary stance coincided with crowding out. However, the crowding out stemmed, not from the expansionary stance itself, but from the way in which it was financed. Funds were transferred to the public sector and the resulting excess demand pushed interest rates up. This tended to crowd out private spending. The phenomenal increase in credit to government of $59.0 million in 1974 withdrew funds normally available to the private sector. Despite such heavy spending government contributed little to growth, in a situation where potential investment funds were transferred to the public sector, thus crowding out the private sector.

The simultaneous increase in public sector credit and interest rates in 1973 and 1974 suggests that commercial rates were bid up by pressure on credit. (This was accentuated by high rates on foreign markets.) Deficit financing therefore tended to compete with the country's growth objectives in 1973, not only by making investment funds difficult to obtain but also by raising the cost of credit. The development of capital markets in the 1980s and 1990s meant that less emphasis was being placed on crowding out since investors tended to directly place funds in government securities and there was consequently less dependence on the banks to fund government deficits.

Government's ability to borrow on the foreign markets also tended to reduce crowding out possibilities during the later period, 1976–1998. Indeed, very often, there was excess liquidity in the system in search of investment opportunities so that the demand for government securities stemmed less from government's needs as from the need for investment instruments by the private sector, particularly by institutional investors. This was particularly so in the post-1992 period.

## FISCAL POLICY AND THE EFFECT OF INFLATION

It has been demonstrated by the case of 1973 when the domestic economy financed government heavily, that fiscal policy did nothing to alleviate inflation. Indeed, it has been argued (Lewis, 1969) that the occurrence of a budget deficit will necessarily lead to inflation, and by others that a budget deficit will be inflationary even if budgets are balanced over time.

In later years (in the 1990s), many central banks, particularly in developed countries, utilized the approach of targeting inflation. They argue that targeting inflation is more effective than targeting credit or the exchange rate, since it shifts the focus of attention to all factors which must cooperate in order to achieve an inflation target. Thus, fiscal policy, interest rate policy and increasingly, wages policy are also seen overtly to play their role and hence, it is argued, a cooperative approach to economic management is more easily achieved.

In a simple linear model of an open economy, Milton Iyoha (1975) suggests, in an examination of fiscally generated inflation, that a budget deficit will be inflationary if government's marginal propensity to spend out of income in the modern sector (the nonagricultural sector) exceeds the marginal tax rate in that sector. He suggests that a way to cure the inflation is to attempt to raise the marginal tax rate in the modern sector and/or begin to tax the subsistence sector. He ignores completely the financing factor as an agent of inflation.

Except for the case of 1973, data for Barbados do not indicate any high degree of fiscally generated inflation. In fact, up to the time of the depreciation of the Barbados currency in 1967 (linked to the pound sterling decline), price rises on an annual basis were small and so were budget deficits. In that period prices were rising at no more than 3% per annum. Inflation rates rose in the post-depreciation period to an average of 8.1% per annum. Budget deficits did not, however, increase particularly (except in 1972). In 1973–1975 budget deficits were large, but most of the inflation was externally generated (because of the rise in oil prices).

However, in 1976, when the budget deficit was excessively large, world inflation was down and domestic prices rose only 7.8% compared with 22.6% in 1974 and 31.9% in 1975. In view of such a small price rise and such a large deficit there seems to be only a limited possibility that fiscally generated inflation could have taken place. A regression of annual rates of inflation on the budget deficits suggests a positive but only mildly significant relationship (see Table 9.3).

Budgetary policy in 1973 and 1975 tended to exacerbate the effects of inflation. The phasing of company taxes and the consequent doubling of tax payments tended to delay new investment. The output of goods and services fell as a result of reduced investment.

In contrast, in the period 1976–1998 there is a less clear relationship between budget deficits and inflation than in the earlier period. Regression results with a coefficient of correlation of 0.58 show that the relationship was not significant. The only instance of fiscally generated inflation in the latter period was related to the introduction of the VAT in 1997. Taxes were paid on services which had not attracted taxes previously. However this was a onetime increase and thereafter the rate of inflation reverted to rates of approximately 3% or lower. The mild relationship between inflation and the budget deficit in this period may have been helped by lower borrowing costs of public debt both domestically and on the foreign market.

**Table 9.3**
**Results of Regression: Impact of Deficits on Economic Variables, 1950–1976**

Economic growth and the fiscal deficit:

| | | |
|---|---|---|
| Per capita GDP | = | 465.1 - 49.95 |
| D | = | fiscal deficit |
| $R^2$ | = | 0.68 |
| DW | = | 1.18 |
| n | = | 26 (years 1950–1976) |
| $Y_p$ | = | per capita GDP |

Money supply and the deficit, 1950–1976:

| | | |
|---|---|---|
| Ms | = | 28.58 - 1.46D |
| Ms | = | money supply |
| Results   $R^2$ | = | 0.61 |
| DW | = | 0.92 |
| n | = | 27 |
| where  D | = | fiscal deficit (negative) |

Inflation and the deficit:

| | | |
|---|---|---|
| P | = | 80.45 - 3.7D |
| where   D | = | fiscal deficit (negative) |
| P | = | retail prices |
| Results   $R^2$ | = | 0.73 |
| DW | = | 1.61 |
| n | = | 27 |

Balance of trade and the deficit:

| | | |
|---|---|---|
| $B_t$ | = | -35.35 + 4.5D |
| where   $B_t$ | = | the balance of trade |
| D | = | the fiscal deficit |
| Results   $R^2$ | = | 73.18 |
| DW | = | 0.54 |
| n | = | 27 |

## FISCAL POLICY AND ITS EFFECT ON THE MONEY SUPPLY

A rapidly growing debt and a large monetization of it can be assumed to be sufficient conditions for fiscally generated inflation, since the budget deficit accelerates the inflationary process if it is financed by high-powered money. This monetarist view holds that the way the budget deficit is financed makes a marked difference to the way the economy is affected in the final analysis. In the period prior to the establishment of the Central Bank this monetization was unlikely.

The years of sharp increases in the money supply in the pre-1970 period were 1951, 1965, 1966 and 1968. These were, however, years of particularly large deficits.[8] This indicates "a priori" little correlation between the deficit and the money supply in this early period. In 1973, a year in which there was some monetization of the debt—7.4% of the debt was monetized[9]—money supply actually declined. Yet, both inflation rates and the fiscal deficit increased substantially. The deficit did not therefore lead to increased money supply and higher inflation in that year. Indeed, the 19.4% increase in GDP suggests that any monetization was matched by increases in output.

In 1974, however, when the deficit was again large and partly monetized, money supply rose significantly, 17.1%. At the same time the rate of inflation rose 31.9%. The deficit seemed not only to lead to increased money supply but the monetization was inflationary. In 1975 and 1976 there was no significant degree of monetization by the Central Bank, and the money supply slowed only slightly from its former rate of growth. Inflation rates slowed.

Purchases of securities in 1975 and 1976 out of excess reserves of the banking system led to increases in bank deposits and hence money supply. These purchases put money into the system that would not otherwise have been available. Hence though the Central Bank did not directly monetize the debt by providing credit directly through advances to government in these years, a large portion of excess reserves of commercial banks were used to purchase government bills. This could have led to increases in the money supply between 1973 and 1976.

Unlike the period 1950–1976 there was a weak direct relationship between the fiscal deficit and the money supply in the latter period. This relationship became increasingly vague in the 1980s and 1990s. With the tendency to issue domestic debt and greater reliance on foreign borrowing, there was less need for Central Bank credit. The establishment of the Central Bank with its more active means of sourcing funds may have been responsible for the weaker relationship between these variables.

A regression of the fiscal deficit on the money supply turns out to be positive but not particularly significant, with a correlation coefficient of determination of 0.61. Regression results showing the effect of the fiscal deficit on economic growth, the money supply plus the balance of payments for the period 1950–1976 are set out in Table 9.3.

The relationship is not as significant as that between prices and the deficit, but could partly be a result of the predominance of years in the series when there was no Central Bank and hence no potential for monetization.

## THE BUDGET DEFICIT AND THE BALANCE OF PAYMENTS

The "new" Cambridge theory of the budget deficit and the balance of payments was tested for Barbados and was not found to be significant. However, a modified version of the theory was found to be more meaningful. The "new" school suggests a direct relationship between the public sector deficit and the balance of payments on the current account in an open economy. Thus the larger the budget deficit the larger the balance of payments deficit on current account. Accordingly, government can set its budget deficit and predict its current account on the balance of payments by a simple linear relationship (X-M) and T-G). In the identity (S-I) is assumed to be stable and:

$$(X-M) = (S-I) + (T-G)$$

The model suggests that the maintenance of internal balance in the economy requires a balance between domestic expenditure and domestic output. The immediate impact of fiscal policy in this situation falls primarily on internal balances and monetary policy on external balances and the balance of payments. However, in the long run the private sector is expected to show a surplus so that the balance of payments on the current account is the result solely of the public sector deficit or surplus (Baptiste, 1976).

When this theory is tested for the Barbadian case using data from 1964–1976,[10] no close relationship is evident between the budget deficit and the balance of payments on current account. A regression gives a coefficient of determination of 0.54. That is, the budget explains just over half the changes in current account balance. A regression of the budget on the overall balance of payments deficit shows an even more tenuous relationship. The coefficient of determination is only 0.40.

Strangely, the relationship that appears to be more significant is that between the budget deficit and the balance of trade. A large proportion of the government budget is spent on wages and salaries and the country has a high propensity to import. The coefficient of determination between the fiscal deficit and the balance of trade is 0.73. The regression equation is given by:

$$B = -35.35 + 4.51D$$

$$R^2 = 0.73 \qquad D.W = 2.0$$

where

B = the balance of trade deficit

D = the fiscal deficit

Of the three monetary relationships with the fiscal deficit, therefore, the most significant, as the results of the regressions suggest, is the effect of the deficit on the balance of trade. There is a mild effect of the deficit on inflation rates and the effect on the money supply is less significant.

As with other relationships the correlation between the fiscal deficit and the balance of trade (balance of payments data were not available for the full period) was less significant in the later period. The only result worthy of reporting for regression of these variables on the fiscal deficit for the period 1976–1998 was the relationship with inflation. The results are set out here:

Inflation and the deficit

where
P     =      187.0 + 1.46D
P     =      retail prices
$R^2$    =      0.58
DW    =      0.149

n     =     20
D     =     fiscal deficit⌐

## STABILIZATION AND STRUCTURAL ADJUSTMENT PROGRAMS, 1982–1983 AND 1991–1992

Prior to 1982–1983 successive governments had engineered their own stabilization programs by consciously taking procyclical or anticyclical positions as circumstances warranted, though in a less calculated way. They determined when cutbacks were necessary and when spending was affordable. While neutral budget stances might not have been calculated with precision, there was a general appreciation of when this was necessary. Generally, these initiatives were based on an approach which determined what level of revenues and expenditures were required to maintain internal and external balance. They were sometimes accompanied by resort to foreign borrowing, but were without conditionalities. IMF programs however, when they came in the early 1980s, were structured stabilization programs, monitored by the Fund and accompanied by conditionalities and penalties for nonperformance.[11] The first program—in 1981–1983—was a combination of a stand-by and a compensatory financing facility which arose as a result of shortfalls in sugar receipts which had created foreign exchange shortages. This followed two consecutive years of decline in the tourism sector and a high fiscal deficit in 1981 and less so in 1982. That program required borrowing of $50.5 million from the Fund under an IMF facility for compensatory shortfalls in export earnings and a stand-by facility that lasted until May 1984. The program included performance criteria for the net domestic assets and on banking system credit to government. The Central Bank put in place a policy of credit controls on the personal and distributive sectors and maintained a tight monetary policy that resulted in higher interest rates. While government exercised fiscal discipline during the program there was no official target for the fiscal deficit, no official requirement to cut spending, no requirement for layoffs in the public sector and no requirements relating to public sector payroll. The targets set were very mild in comparison with the 1991–1992 program and with a little national restraint were easily achieved.

The IMF Program entered into by the government of Barbados in 1992 was much more all-encompassing. It sought to stabilize the economy by reducing the fiscal and the balance of payments deficits. It was predicated on the maintenance of the exchange rate of BDS$2 to US$1. Over the short term it required contraction of public spending. The strategy also focused on removing the antiexport bias from manufacturing as the basis for renewed economic growth in the medium term. These objectives were achieved by a reduction in public spending, wage cuts of public servants of the order of 8%, lower public sector employment, reduced transfers to public enterprises and a deferment of some capital works projects. In addition, taxes, including an across-the-board consumption tax of 3% and a 20% luxury tax were put in place. Rents of government-owned units were increased and water rates and bus fares were raised.

On the monetary side, higher interest rates and liquidity requirements for banks were introduced to dampen private sector spending. To encourage investment in export-oriented activities, measures were introduced to reduce the bias toward import substitution. It is noted that IMF and IBRD programs do tend to have a certain philosophy and the reduction of the antiexport bias and the removal of concessions to domestic manufacturing tend to be among these philosophies. To enhance competitiveness, the government announced its desire to see a freeze on basic wages in the private sector. Had it been possible to achieve a reduction in wages of the same order of 8% in the private sector, the objective of improving competitiveness would have been achieved, thereby enhancing the ability of Barbadian manufacturers to sell outside of Barbados. However, the 8% reduction in the wages of public servants was at best an indication of what ought to have happened in the private sector and to that extent it was very important. However, a historic agreement referred to as Protocol I was agreed with the private sector, government and labor unions who agreed to freeze wages for 18 months. While the desired reduction in private sector wages was not achieved, the freeze in wages was itself a significant achievement. The fact that the cooperation of labor unions was obtained was a landmark stage in the history of labor unions in Barbados and indeed in the Caribbean. The program hinged on the achievement of a reduction in public and private sector demand. It was able to achieve the public sector cutback but stopped short of reaching agreement on an across the board wage reduction which would have further reduced private sector demand and improved competitiveness.

The plan outlined above, termed the IMF program, was supported by borrowing from the Fund and from the World Bank and the IADB. A letter of intent verifying the country's commitment to an 18-month adjustment program with the backing of the IMF was agreed. The first drawing was of the order of US$41 million or BDS$82 million in the last quarter of the calendar year. Subsequent drawings were made quarterly on successful completion of certain agreed performance criteria. These criteria involved the meeting of certain targets on central government deficits, borrowing requirements of the consolidated public sector, an agreed level of net domestic assets of the Central Bank, net international reserves of the Central Bank and a limit on net accumulation of external debt by the public sector.

The burden of adjustment fell on fiscal and monetary policy as government opted to use no exchange rate adjustment. The program was therefore designed to achieve these targets and a level of stabilization in fiscal and monetary accounts and in the balance of payments, while keeping the exchange rate stable. This explains why the order of adjustment was that severe. That was a consequence of opting to use principally two tools and not three, that is, monetary and fiscal policy and not exchange rate policy. It meant that the order of magnitude of the changes required in monetary and fiscal policy were therefore larger.

The program was front-loaded in terms of adjustment and in terms of funding. Barbados received BDS$82 million up front and small amounts quarterly thereafter. In the same way, most of the measures were taken up front. Very few measures were left to be put in place after the first disbursement. This gave both the IMF and the public some reassurance, the IMF as to implementation and the public as to relief from further impositions. It also helped to give some comfort to businesspeople and the private sector generally and allowed them to plan for the future without uncertainties about what was likely to happen next.

As a consequence of the fiscal and monetary adjustment, the government was able to achieve a fiscal deficit to GDP ratio of 1% in 1992, down from a trend figure in excess of 8% which had been projected for the year in the absence of adjustment measures. This led to a reduction in the level of net domestic assets—principally credit to government and the commercial banks. By mid-1992, net international reserves had increased and by year-end were BDS$42.1 million. Increases in the net international reserves were achieved through dampening demand and through measures to reduce disposable incomes and increase committed incomes. (The term "committed incomes" refers to commitments to mortgage payment and loan payments which would have increased as a result of higher interest rates and other charges.)

Spending patterns took some time to be adjusted and until this was accomplished, savings tended to be withdrawn from the banking system as individuals made attempts to meet outstanding commitments based on planned disposable incomes. Pressure on credit continued for some time until spending habits adjusted to the lower disposable incomes, declining by the end of 1992. The strong influence of North American attitudes, styles and consumption habits made adjustment of spending habits difficult. Policy tools such as credit and interest rate controls were necessary because it was judged that cultural penetration had made it impossible to appeal to qualities of thrift for which Barbadians had been known over the years. Credit controls, increased interest rates and increased charges were used to bring about the desired changes in the spending habits of the consumer. The savings habit was encouraged through an increase in interest rates. The minimum savings rate was raised and the weighted average lending rate was lifted.

In this scenario, commercial banks also needed to adjust. In a small society where bankers know their customers and have established personal friendships with them it was very difficult for banks to deny them credit, especially those who were prime customers. Particular difficulty was experienced with credit to the distributive sector. In large economies where there is greater anonymity, credit cutbacks are less difficult to achieve. It was eventually achieved but with great difficulty.

In the process it was necessary to work on the assumption that many Barbadians held that a high standard of living was necessarily the most important goal. It was necessary to convey the fact that Barbados' standard of living was among the higher levels attained in the developing world as reported in UNDP reports. This carried its own implications for costs and for competitiveness. In ensuring consumer acceptance of the program it was important to convey to the consuming public that it was necessary to ensure that the standard of living was consistent with the foreign exchange resources which the community had at its disposal. The view that maintenance of a high standard of living also had certain macroeconomic costs had to be understood.

Labor unions were brought into the planning process and economic development goal setting. They were required to rethink their positions on their role as bargainers for higher incomes and higher wages. They needed to see that the long-term consequences for the labor force of pressuring businesses to pay higher wages could mean the closure of the businesses themselves and the layoff of workers. It was recognized that Barbados had to amend its labor laws. This it was felt was in critical need of adjustment, so that companies could be given more flexibility in planning expansion programs which required staff reductions, and which permitted them to more easily exit one activity and enter another, since it was often more costly for companies to close than to continue in operation. Barbados seemed to have gone overboard in compensating displaced employees and had not paid sufficient attention to the resulting viability of businesses, and had not appreciated that the ability of business to continue to employ was contingent on that business' ability to meet its costs, and that if these costs are too high—and labor costs tend to form a large proportion of total costs—then the entire business is threatened and the employment of the work force as well.

As a consequence of higher interest rates, higher consumption taxes, higher payroll taxes and other costs, water rates and bus fares; inflation rates rose in late 1991 and into 1992. Since many of these measures were, however, one-time measures, the inflation rate moderated late in 1993. However, there were secondary impacts of these increased costs in the form of higher prices as businesses adjusted to the higher cost of imported inputs.

In the short term, interest rates rose as commercial banks tried to meet new securities requirements. This proved a little difficult in the short run until banks adjusted the level of private sector credit. In order to meet securities requirements they had either to attract new deposits or wind down credit. Since to some extent banks had committed themselves to certain levels of credit, winding down was difficult. In a situation where individuals were drawing down deposits, that added another dimension to their ability to meet reserve requirements, but this too worked itself through the system in the months following the beginning of the program.

Interest rates rose as commercial banks tried to attract additional funds, but the pressure to raise rates eased as the criteria were satisfied. Indeed given the measures that government undertook and its commitment to reduce the fiscal deficit to 1% of GDP, credit to government from the banking system declined, leaving greater leeway for private sector credit to increase by 1993. The greatest effort toward reduction of the deficit was required in 1991/1992, the reduction in 1992/1993 being considerably smaller. By 1992/1993 it was anticipated that the pressure on government would have eased and the ability of the private sector to access credit would have improved.

The program was intended to achieve a one-third reduction in debt service obligations form the peak levels experienced in 1990 and 1991, since high debt service obligations—largely bullet loans—were partly responsible for the poor foreign exchange situation that necessitated the program. In the short term, therefore, government needed to absorb a larger share of savings in order to meet its debt obligations—but by 1992 the country's debt service obligations had reached manageable proportions. New debt assumed in 1992 was less than amortizations, exclusive of IMF debt, so that the country's debt service obligations declined. The country's ability to keep acquisition of new debt within its ability to service meant continued restraint in government spending—even beyond the program period. Continued restraint needed to be tempered in later years in order to permit the economy to grow. Positive growth was programmed for 1992—but this did not materialize.

Avoiding arrears in debt service was the single most important factor in gaining access to capital markets. While Barbados was able to make some accommodation for a Japanese loan repayment without adverse implications for credibility in the market, it was not a desired option, since the country's reputation in the market is integrally linked with its ability to service debt as it falls due.

Unemployment was one of the major problems of the program. With a labor force in the region of 123,000 persons at the time, a 1% increase in unemployment was approximately the layoff of 1,200 odd persons. Layoffs of over 3,000 persons in the government sector added two and a half percentage points to the unemployment rate. However, unemployment in the private sector also increased as was expected in a year of negative growth and there was no possibility of stimulating the private sector through new credit. In addition, lower disposable incomes and cutbacks in spending had adverse implications for employment. Also, the cutback in government servants' salaries would have led to a reduction in sales volumes, particularly in the distributive sector.

Prior to the announcement of the program and during the period of foreign exchange rationing there was pre-buying and hoarding of inventory. This meant that the normal relationship of imports to sales would have been distorted, as much of the inventory would appear in imports but would not be reflected in sales until some time after. The expectation of the program was that the deficit on the balance of payments should reverse in 1992 and 1993 and beyond. The expectation also was that there must continue to be some restraint in spending and that wages settlements would continue to be controlled. During the program period the tourism sector was the sector on which the country depended for foreign exchange earnings and to increase output. This was possible since visitors were not affected by local developments and decisions to travel did not take into account domestic economic problems. On the distribution side, despite the build-up in inventory, there was still a decline in output in the distributive trades in 1991 and this was more marked in 1992.

Nonsugar output was somewhat down in 1991, but positive for 1992. However, the future of the sugar industry was an important factor in the restructuring exercise and in the Fund program. The offshore sector was not a major issue in the Fund program. It was clear, however, that while there were foreign exchange and revenue possibilities from that sector the likely impact on employment was limited.

In the medium term it was important for there to be some level of restraint. It was important that labor unions refrained from feeding demand through increased wages. Wage restraint was important not only to dampen inflationary impact but also to improve competitiveness. When one uses all three policy tools (monetary fiscal and exchange rate) one is able to achieve competitiveness provided the labor unions help in the effort to reduce or control the inflation rate. In the 1991–1992 situation, only two policy tools were used and the country needed the cooperation of the labor unions to an even greater extent, in order to improve competitiveness.

Efforts were made during this period to review the role of government. The point was made that government was to be seen as a facilitator, as a planner, as the institution that provides the framework in which the private sector operates, but it should not be the institution which keeps the wheels of commerce turning. Barbados had to rethink the view put abroad, mostly by governments themselves, that governments were there to provide jobs, incomes and services. As a result the country found itself with a dependency attitude which needed to be corrected. Governments owed it to themselves not to put abroad that kind of view. There was a time when it was necessary for government to provide many basic services. But incomes had risen over time and the period of structural adjustment served as a time to rethink the role of government. Though there was some rollback, but it proved very difficult for government to roll back certain of the services it had previously provided or to introduce user charges, though some headway was made during the period.

Government also accepted the position of the IMF that several statutory corporations should be privatized so as to bring the size of the government sector under control. The prime candidates for privatization were those that produced goods. It proved more difficult to privatize those that produced services, largely because there was a certain social necessity to provide services to the lower-income groups. In some countries however, in Latin America for example, methods have been found whereby these enterprises have been privatized. This does not mean that there is not a role for government involvement in what would normally be termed "private sector activities." It might be argued that government should in fact be facilitating this, particularly in the case of large enterprises which require massive investment, massive amounts of technology and know-how which might not be otherwise available to small companies in the private sector.

One of the other lessons that was learnt from the experience of the structural adjustment program of 1991–1992 was that there needed to be some commercialization in the government. This had to do with improvement in the level of efficiency both in the government service and in the statutory boards. The term "commercialization" is more meaningful than the term privatization here, since it speaks to government's commitment to continue to provide many of the basic services—economic, social and otherwise—while ensuring a commercial approach to provision of these services, both in terms of improved productivity and efficiency in those enterprises.

The tax system was also an ingredient of the structural adjustment program. Discussions about bringing about a change in the system centered on encouraging persons to move out of real estate and into productive activity. However, there was not much measurable progress in this area.

In the second phase of discussion with IADB, government was cautioned by several sources to ensure that liberalization programs which are normally the philosophy of many international financing institutions did not frustrate the long-term objectives of growth and development.

The provision of the IMF funding helped to provide the confidence to consumers that foreign exchange would be available and so assisted in arresting the tendency to hoard foreign exchange. It also helped to encourage hoarders to turn in foreign exchange already hoarded and helped to alleviate some of the cash flow problems that resulted from hoarding.

Government and the public were encouraged to use the opportunity of the IMF program to rethink the role of government, to rethink whether it was appropriate to burden government with a large payroll and to pressure government to continually increase wages, and to rethink whether it was in the best interests of the country to expect government to be the major employer. Consumers were also cautioned that it was important for

Barbados to keep the demand for foreign exchange within its ability to earn foreign exchange and to live within its foreign exchange earning capability.


## SUMMARY AND CONCLUSION

The structure of the economy, the size of the country and the stage of economic development strongly influenced fiscal policy choices during each stabilization period. Expenditure on wages, transfers to households and tended to be regressive and to have a pro-poor bias and were considered inflexible until 1992. The capacity of government to absorb funds for capital projects was sometimes limited and adversely affected gross capital formation in the public sector.

Expenditure and tax changes were sufficient to stabilize the economy only when the required changes were small or moderate. This also depended on taxable capacity. Taxable capacity increased significantly in real terms and tax effort fluctuated, sometimes sharply but the economy was undertaxed to a lesser extent than it was overtaxed. The balance struck was between protecting the balance of payments and increasing the tax take. Similarly, there was a trade-off between increased corporate investment and higher company tax receipts.

Fiscal performance suggested that there was scope for stabilization policies despite inflexibilities in expenditure, but there was the danger of such policies being counterproductive. High levels of spending did not necessarily lead to higher rates of economic growth; rather, expansionary budgets caused by tax cuts had a greater propensity to result in higher rates of growth than expansionary budgets fueled by spending.

The rate of growth in foreign debt exceeded the rate at which the country earned foreign exchange during some periods. It was therefore imperative that foreign funds be placed in foreign-exchange-generating projects. The relationship between the deficit and the balance of trade was positive and significant. Fiscal deficits tended to affect inflation rates to a lesser extent. The effect of the deficit on the money supply was surprisingly less significant. It would have been expected that after the establishment of the Central Bank the relationship would have become more marked. The explanation may lie in the use of the foreign credit markets.

Finally, the outlook for the performance of the public sector hinged on the size of the deficit. Where these deficits were not being controlled, the pattern of expenditure needed to be adjusted to one that would encourage economic growth. That is, expenditure should be productive and foreign-exchange-generating and should be made in full cognizance of the possible effect on the economy. Such changes, given certain inflexibilities could necessitate a restructuring of the economy and a new role for the government sector.

Approaches to stabilization during the first twenty-five-year period of the study were completely different from stabilization approaches in the later period. Demand management, foreign exchange adequacy and a fiscal system which were self-sustaining were the main objectives of stabilization policies of the1980s and 1990s. In the second phase, monetary policy and monetary management were inextricably linked to fiscal stabilization as interest rate and credit policy were critical dimensions of demand management which had been absent from the fiscal stabilization policies of the pre-1975 period.

By far the most significant development of the second stabilization period was the role played by fiscal policy through the raising of taxes, cuts in public sector wages and cuts in the public sector payroll in 1992. This was unprecedented and effective and was instrumental in effecting stabilization of the economy within a reasonably short period. The significance of the program for overturing conventional IMF prescriptions was quite impressive and its success was noted by others. In comparing the economies of Barbados and Hong Kong the journal "Credit Week" notes similarities in these two infrequently compared economies. The article, Mukerji (2000) notes that Barbados undertook an impressive array of reforms in response to balance of payments crisis in 1991, largely through government supported policies designed to reduce consumption and income. These measures achieved the objective.

**NOTES**

1. This is a simple model and does not allow expenditure and revenue to be weighted.

2. References in this section to GDP will refer to GDP in current prices.

3. Prices had until then been rising at an annual rate of under 5% (except in 1951 and 1952 when the change in the basket of goods in the retail price index was altered.)

4. The country had been fortunate to obtain bonanza sugar prices in 1974 and fairly high prices in 1975 as well.

5. Dissaving is measured by the excess of current expenditure over current revenue.

6. This stipulation at first applied to treasury bills only, but later debentures were included.

7. Under the East Caribbean currency system, the fact that the monetary authority was regional and that it had to maintain 90% of its currency liabilities in United Kingdom assets precluded the monetization of debt.

8. The largest deficit in this period was in 1968 when the deficit was $10.0 million in current prices.

9. In addition, several purchases of government securities were made by the Central Bank. Such purchases normally increase bank deposits and hence money supply. Where such increases are not matched by commensurate increases in goods and services, they can be inflationary.

10. No balance of payments data are available prior to 1964.

11. These penalties related to eligibility for future-promised drawings.

# 10

## Debt Management

### INTRODUCTION

Debt management is a central component of fiscal management. It has important implications for current costs and future obligations and impacts on both domestic and external creditors. Hence its impact on confidence and on fiscal stability is critical. This chapter examines the evolution of the national debt and evaluates its impact on macroeconomic performance, on savings and on stabilization policies. It also evaluates the management of debt maturities and discusses the implications of debt issues for private sector access to credit.

It focuses on the role played by statutory government securities requirements, and addresses the role of the Central Bank in managing liquidity and pricing of securities in that context. The chapter also discusses the lack of depth in the market in securities and the part played by open market operations in developing such depth. It emphasizes the role of reserve requirements in the reaction function of policy makers and concludes that securities requirements, though managed by the Central Bank, tended to be more a fiscal than a monetary tool. Regression analysis is utilized to test the relationship between reserve requirements and key economic variables. These show a strong relationship between explanatory variables and the policy decision to use reserve requirements as a tool of macroeconomic management.

A special section is devoted to the potential role of the regional securities market and the opportunity it offers for improving the management of debt. The need for second-tier balance of payments support access, so as to avoid resort to borrowing from the international financial institutions is discussed in that context.

Government's entrance into the foreign markets, the role of credit ratings and the international trends toward use of private sector ratings by international financial institutions is discussed in the light of the evolving new global financial architecture.

The basic measure of the level of indebtedness used is the ratio of debt outstanding to GDP or to exports of goods and services (see Table 10.1). The first ratio rose from 5.3% in 1950, to 38.2% in 1976 and to 76.3% in 1998. When the level of foreign indebtedness is measured by the ratio of foreign debt service to exports of goods and services, the rise is also quite marked. Despite the increasing importance of domestic debt this ratio rocketed from 1.7% in 1976, to 14.7% in 1994, falling to 6.7% in 1997 (see Table 10.1). The increase indicates that debt servicing (which normally increases as debt rises) represented, up to the late 1990s, an increasingly greater proportion of export earnings (see Table 10.1). This was the result of a change in the stance of government toward development financing.

## CHANGING PATTERNS IN DEBT MANAGEMENT, 1950–1973

In the period 1950–1973, with the exception of 1950–1955 and 1968, when government turned out mostly small surpluses, deficit financing had become increasingly the regular pattern. Persistent deficits led to rapid increases in national debt. Debt rose by an annual average of 19.4% per annum in the 24 years reviewed (see Table 10.2). In the very early years, the period 1950–1959, the national debt had remained quite low, but rose sharply after a loan to finance the Deep Water Harbor was secured, and continued a steady rise since that time.

The historical development of financing patterns is closely linked to the level of development. The difficulties of placing government debt in the domestic market in the early 1960s sprang mainly from the insufficiency of savings and the limited development of financial institutions. Unused cash balances of public sector entities were first tapped (The Labor Welfare Fund, the Sugar Funds and Special Funds). Later, with the establishment of a social security scheme, and with the development of the Government Savings Bank, these institutions became large holders of government debt. Purchases of debt by commercial banks were minimal, and dependent mainly on the demand in the private sector and interest rates abroad (since funds were at this time being exported) and on the level of liquidity in the system. In 1973, in addition to the requirement that commercial banks hold a fixed percentage of their liabilities in government securities (local securities ratio of commercial banks), Exchange Control Regulations were tightened. This put an end to capital flight so that locally held loanable funds were made available to government both on a voluntary and on a compulsory basis. In times of excess liquidity, since funds could no longer be exported, government became the beneficiary of credit from the private sector.

**Table 10.1**

**Selected Debt Ratios, 1950–1998**

| Period | Domestic debt as a % of GDP | Total debt as a % of GDP | Debt service as a % of revenue | Foreign debt service as a % of exports of goods & services | Total debt service as a % of exports good & services |
|--------|------|------|------|------|------|
| 1950 | .. | 5.3 | .. | .. | .. |
| 1958 | 8.6 | .. | .. | .. | .. |
| 1965 | .. | 27.3 | 8.3 | .. | .. |
| 1970 | 14.1 | 24.5 | 7.6 | 1.0 | 1.6 |
| 1975 | 22.6 | 28.8 | 9.8 | 1.5 | 2.5 |
| 1980 | 21.4 | 32.1 | 11.8 | 2.0 | 3.2 |
| 1985 | 29.9 | 50.2 | 16.6 | 3.9 | 4.7 |
| 1990 | 34.4 | 62.6 | 23.5 | 7.4 | 7.3 |
| 1995 | 56.2 | 76.9 | 32.0 | 6.1 | 10.8 |
| 1998 | 58.2 | 76.3 | 27.3 | 5.7 | 10.2 |

*Sources*: Central Bank of Barbados, annual statistical digest and balance of payments of Barbados.

The government deficit was almost totally bond financed up to 1973. With the start of active operation of the Central Bank, the Bank became potentially an expansionary source of government borrowing since money lent to government by Central Banks serve to raise the reserves of the commercial banks and provide a base for multiple expansion of their credit (Levin, 1970). However, in this early period, the deficit was partly financed by the Central Bank only in 1973 and 1974 and then only to a limited extent of $3.4 million and $10.3 million.

**Table 10.2**
**Structure of National Debt, 1950–1975**

| Period | Domestic short-term | Domestic long-term | Total domestic | Total foreign | Total debt |
|--------|---------------------|--------------------|----------------|---------------|------------|
| 1950   | ..                  | ..                 | ..             | ..            | 2.9        |
| 1955   | ..                  | ..                 | ..             | ..            | 4.9        |
| 1958   | ..                  | ..                 | ..             | ..            | 9.7        |
| 1959   | ..                  | ..                 | ..             | ..            | 23.6       |
| 1965   | ..                  | ..                 | ..             | ..            | 43.2       |
| 1966   | 0.5                 | 20.5               | 21             | 25.7          | 46.5       |
| 1967   | 1.8                 | 22.1               | 23.9           | 28.2          | 52.1       |
| 1968   | 7.5                 | 23.7               | 31.2           | 30.2          | 61.4       |
| 1969   | 8.1                 | 24.7               | 32.8           | 30.2          | 63         |
| 1970   | 9.3                 | 31.5               | 40.8           | 30.2          | 71         |
| 1971   | 19.7                | 31.5               | 51.2           | 30.2          | 81.4       |
| 1972   | 22.1                | 49.9               | 71.9           | 32.1          | 104        |
| 1975   | 21.6                | 56.2               | 77.8           | 55.4          | 133.2      |

*Sources*: Central Bank of Barbados, annual statistical digests.

A large proportion of government's debt tended to be financed by short-term credit. Whereas in 1950, all government debt was long-term; as from 1967 the use of short-term debt increased continually and by 1975, 40.5% of domestic debt was short-term. All short-term debt was domestic at that time. This was indicative of the reluctance of local purchasers to enter long-term commitments. It reflected the absence of an active market in claims and securities, and was also a consequence of an ad hoc element in government planning.

A cycle can be observed in the holding of domestic debt. Government moved from having all its debt being held domestically to just over half held domestically during the mid-1960s, and by 1976, reverted to a situation where up to 80.6% of debt was domestic, very similar to the position 16 years earlier. The shift to greater domestic borrowing marked the end of a period when access to the capital markets of the United Kingdom was open and the island still had colonial status. Foreign loans outstanding grew slowly at first, rising in the post-1970 period from $25.7 million in 1970 where it stayed for five years to $50.2 million in 1976. This slow rate of foreign borrowing for project loans tended to be commensurate with the country's ability to prepare and carry out investment rather than a function of its capacity to repay.

## DEBT SERVICING, 1950–1973

Like most developing countries Barbados' debt burden grew relatively rapidly so that refinancing of domestic debt became quite standard. Total debt grew at an annual average rate of 19.4% and exports (an indicator of the ability to earn foreign exchange) at an annual rate of 9.1%. A comparison shows that the national debt of developing countries with similar per capita incomes grew at an annual rate of 17.5% and exports at 7.3%, slightly below the average in both cases. The Barbados rate of growth of debt and its financing capabilities were therefore both above average. In 1965 debt service payments represented 8.3% of revenue compared with 15.0% in 1972. However, a large percentage of debt was domestic and therefore was no charge on the foreign exchange reserves.

The process of securing a net transfer by obtaining new loans in excess of debt servicing obligations, referred to as the rollover process, can be used as an indicator of the proportion of disbursements that appear to service the debt (Levin, 1970). Data on gross disbursements are not available for the entire period. However, net disbursements were on average 2.5 times the cost of servicing the debt in the period 1950–1965 and fell to 2.0 times that cost in the 10-year period 1966–1976.

It is often argued that the burden of the debt is paid, not by the borrowers but by those from whom funds are diverted to the government. Based on this argument, in 1973 when liquidity in the system was low and funds were diverted from the private sector to government (through stipulated investment in government securities) the increased debt tended to be a burden to the extent that potential borrowers paid an inflation tax by being forced to postpone the use of these funds until a time when their real value would have been eroded by inflation. This was particularly so in 1973 and 1974 when prices rose sharply. It can be argued that the private sector bore the burden of the debt in those years.

## INFLATION AND THE DEBT, 1950–1973

Inflation lightened the burden of the debt from government's perspective and partly offset its negative effects. The sharp price rises of 1973 and 1974 helped to shrink previous debt accumulation and the continuing depreciation of the BDS dollar (the pound sterling was falling) also reduced the value of debt repayments denominated in sterling. The responsibility for redeeming such a large debt should not therefore have burdened future generations to any great extent.[1]

The shift to domestic debt and the consequent easing of the debt burden was associated with government's holding a smaller proportion of sinking funds as a contingency against the national debt. In the nine-year period 1950–1959, the ratio of sinking funds to total debt was quite high, between 25% and 75% of gross debt, but declined to 4.7% of total debt by 1976 when rolling over became the norm. The lower level of contingency funds was a result of the predominance of domestic debt and the tendency to repay old debt by the acquisition of new debt.

## DOMESTIC DEBT AND STABILIZATION, 1973–1993

During the period 1973–1993 borrowing was seen as a means of financing higher levels of economic development. This appeared to be the approach up to the period of the second stabilization program. Indeed, Keynesian views and structuralist views of third world economists combined to influence successive governments into taking an active role in promoting accelerated economic development. This approach contributed to rapid growth of government debt in the 1970s and 1980s.

The period 1973–1993 also witnessed uneven fiscal performances. Government experienced wide swings in performance, culminating in the structural adjustment program with the IMF of 1991–1992 which was itself preceded by a period of debt management with a focus on stabilization. The period 1973–1993 was in fact most varied in terms of debt management.

The next section examines the growth of domestic debt in Barbados over that volatile 20-year period 1973–1993 and assesses the implications for economic stabilization.[2]

It first describes general trends in both domestic and foreign debt, secondly, it examines some of the issues and the adjustment procedures in managing debt and thirdly, it looks at the challenges to the management of domestic debt which faced Barbados during this period—a period which saw the country entering two IMF programs.

## GROWTH OF DOMESTIC DEBT, 1973–1993

In Barbados, as in most developing countries, the view was widely held that governments needed to take an active role in promoting economic development and until the 1980s, the size of the government sector was not seen as problematic. As a result, government spending rose rapidly and so did the national debt (see Figure 10.1). Increasingly, as repayment became more onerous, it became clear that the burden of debt was a future cost that would sooner or later have to be met and should be taken into account "ex ante" into payment scheduling if repayment was to be assured.

**Figure 10.1**

**Growth of Domestic Debt and Securitized Debt**

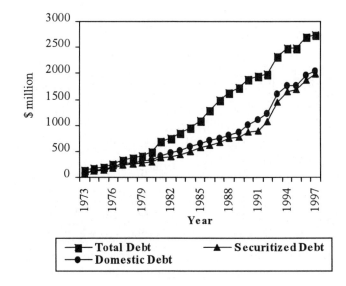

Domestic debt in Barbados grew over 20-fold during the 20-year period 1973–1993. During this period foreign debt rose rapidly as well. The share of domestic debt in total debt averaged 65% and was at its highest during the period 1974–1979 when it represented approximately three-quarters of total debt. This was attributable principally to securitized debt. The highest level thereafter was in 1993 when domestic debt represented 71% of total debt (see Figure 10.1). The shift in the share of domestic debt in total debt in the intervening period is attributable, not to a decline in net issues of domestic debt, but to increased issues of foreign debt. During the period the ratio of foreign debt to GDP rose from 25% of GDP to 58% in 1993 and represented 16% of revenue compared to 8% in 1983 and 6% in 1973.

Figure 10.1 shows that total debt rose faster than domestic debt in the period 1980–1988 as government made increasing use of the foreign bond markets.[3]    Data also demonstrate that most of domestic debt was securitized though there was an increase in unsecuritized debt in the period 1989–1991 as government resorted to increased use of its overdraft with the Central Bank.

## FISCAL DEFICITS AND NEW ISSUES

Increases in domestic debt were fueled by large fiscal deficits. In seven out of the 20 years (1973–1993) the fiscal deficit exceeded 20% of total expenditure. Massive deficits were recorded in 1973/1974 and 1977/1978 when fiscal deficits exceeded 25% of expenditure and were funded principally from domestic sources.    Fiscal deficits tended to mirror new debt issues until 1990–1992 when they declined sharply as the country embarked on a structural adjustment program.  Domestic debt increased partly in response to a decline in foreign debt (see Figure 10.2) and partly because of the restructuring of government operations. (Legal limits were set on the issue of domestic debt and were revised periodically according to the financing needs of government and rarely took account of the macroeconomic considerations of deficit financing.[4])    This placed considerable burden on monetary policy.

In 1981 the fiscal deficit rose to 9% of GDP subsequent to government's entering an IMF program and again to 8.3% of GDP in 1990, just prior to its entering another.  Both of these occasions precipitated a decline in reserves causing the country to enter stabilization programs and were largely attributable to major debt servicing difficulties. While the impact of a large foreign debt is clearly seen in a reduction in reserves through debt servicing costs, the impact of servicing domestic debt tends to be underestimated because its impact is not as immediate and the result in terms of reserve loss tends to take longer to work itself through the system. But it nevertheless contributes to spending and hence indirectly to a decline in reserves where these finance such spending.

**Figure 10.2**
**Domestic Debt and the Fiscal Deficit**

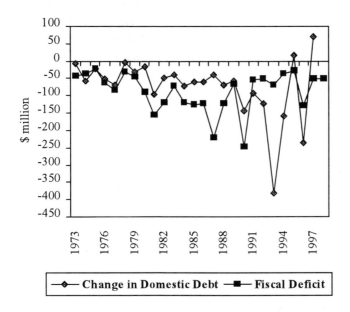

## MATURITY STRUCTURE OF DOMESTIC DEBT

Maturities of domestic debt shortened over the period 1973–1993 (see Tables 10.3 and 10.4). Debt issued in the pre-1973 period carried considerably longer maturities, ranging from 12 to 35 years, with the majority of debt carrying maturities in excess of 20 years. With the uncertainty in international exchange rates and interest rates that followed the post-1971 period, and the floating of sterling to which the Barbados dollar was tied, maturities of domestic securities mirrored those of international securities, becoming considerably shorter. Consequently, in the post-1973 period securities with maturities of 20 years or over were never again issued until 21 years later when government converted a contingent liability into a securitized loan.[5] The tendency for domestic debt to be medium to long-term between 1981 and 1985 was followed by a period of inordinate dependence on short-term domestic debt, with maturities becoming even shorter, reflecting increased pressures of deficit financing. This illustrates that the problems that eventually surfaced in 1990/1991, which resulted in an IMF program, really had their genesis in the 1980s.

The declared objective of foreign borrowing in the 1982–1985 period was to build up a store of foreign exchange to finance restructuring of the productive sectors. This objective was not achieved. Domestic and foreign debt rose rapidly and simultaneously. No success was achieved in reducing issues of domestic debt while government was negotiating aggressively on the foreign markets. Government relied increasingly on Central Bank financing in the late 1980s and into 1990. During the periods of rapidly increasing foreign debt, total short-term domestic debt failed to decline and was reflected principally in high levels on overdraft facilities with the Central Bank. Indeed, domestic debt on an annual basis did not decline at any time over that 20-year period. In 1991 the government finally yielded to financing pressures and increased the limit on overdraft facilities available from the Central Bank from 10% of current revenues to 17.5%.

This introduced concerns about the independence of the Central Bank and the related concerns of whether the Central Bank was a passive actor merely supplying government with credit. While there was considerably greater fiscal restraint in the period following the country's entry into a Fund program, this question remained unresolved until 1992 when the statutory limit on advances to government by the Central Bank by way of ways and means advances was again reduced to 10% of current revenue of government.

New instruments were placed on the market to attract financing and to encourage saving. Medium-term debt instruments in the form of savings bonds and treasury notes were launched in the 1980—savings bonds in 1981 and treasury notes in 1989 (see Table 10.3). These targeted different markets. Treasury notes were targeted at the institutional investor with a shorter-term horizon than could be satisfied with debenture issues averaging 10 years to maturity, while the savings bond was targeted at individual investors who desired liquidity but were not overly concerned about income flows.[6] The introduction of the savings bond was designed to press individuals into financing the deficit and so reduce reliance on institutional investors. Tax incentives were added to increase the attraction of the savings bond instrument. Interest earnings on savings bonds were tax free up to a maximum holding of $50,000 per person compared with earnings on debentures and treasury bills that carry a tax rate of 12.5%.

During the period of the 1991–1992 Fund program a substantial part of domestic debt continued to be short-term, suggesting a level of urgency in the issuing of new debt. Because of the short lead time needed for the issue of treasury bills and greater flexibility in responding to interest rate changes in the market during this period, the government became increasingly dependent on these 90-day treasury bill issues as a means of financing government expenditure. They were continuously rolled over and formed a hard core of short-term debt.

Up to 1983 when debt was not of very short duration, it tended to be of rather long maturities. There was no middle ground. In 1983, maturities averaged 10–15 years. There were no securities with maturities of 1–5 years and the median range of securities was for periods of 10–15 years. The shortening of maturities is demonstrated in Figures 10.3 and 10.5 which compare 1983 and 1993.

These debts, though of relatively long maturities were due for redemption mostly within the following five-year period 1984–1988, indicating a bunching of debt in that period. This is represented by the period 0–5 years in Figure 10.4 shown by outstanding maturity at December 1983.

**Figure 10.3**

**Domestic Debt-Original Maturity, December 1983**

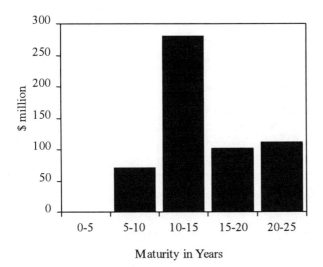

Maturity in Years

**Table 10.3**
**Domestic Debt of Barbados by Instrument, 1973–1993**
$ million

| Period | Treasury bills | Savings bonds | Debentures and treasury notes | Total |
|--------|------|------|------|------|
| 1973 | 18.1 | – | 53.1 | 71.2 |
| 1974 | 47.0 | – | 83.9 | 110.9 |
| 1976 | 94.6 | – | 93.2 | 187.8 |
| 1977 | 114.4 | – | 121.9 | 236.3 |
| 1979 | 149.4 | – | 125.4 | 274.8 |
| 1980 | 164.2 | – | 130.6 | 294.8 |
| 1981 | 228.1 | 2.5 | 143.0 | 373.6 |
| 1982 | 265.6 | 2.4 | 137.8 | 405.8 |
| 1983 | 302.3 | 2.4 | 134.7 | 439.4 |
| 1984 | 350.6 | 4.5 | 139.5 | 494.6 |
| 1985 | 404.9 | 6.9 | 154.7 | 566.5 |
| 1986 | 422.5 | 13.7 | 189.9 | 626.1 |
| 1987 | 423.9 | 21.5 | 234.0 | 680.3 |
| 1988 | 434.0 | 26.0 | 294.4 | 754.4 |
| 1989 | 426.9 | 26.9 | 319.4 | 773.2 |
| 1990 | 506.2 | 34.6 | 341.7 | 882.5 |
| 1991 | 497.7 | 37.1 | 350.7 | 885.5 |
| 1992 | 635.2 | 30.2 | 411.1 | 1,076.5 |
| 1993 | 648.5 | 37.6 | 762.1 | 1,448.2 |

*Sources*: Central Bank of Barbados, annual statistical digests.

**Table 10.4**
**Growth and Share of Domestic Debt in Total Debt, 1973–1993**
$ million

| Period | Domestic debt $ million | Domestic as a % of total | Short-term domestic as a % of total domestic | Growth of total debt (% change) | Growth of short-term domestic (% change) | Fiscal deficit $ million | Total Expenditure $ million | Fiscal deficit as a % of expenditure |
|---|---|---|---|---|---|---|---|---|
| 1973 | 77.8 | 0.58 | 0.16 | .. | .. | -42.3 | 167.5 | 25.3 |
| 1975 | 158.0 | 0.78 | 0.33 | 0.13 | 0.08 | -21.6 | 220.1 | 9.8 |
| 1980 | 329.3 | 0.67 | 0.39 | 0.16 | 0.06 | -89.7 | 530.8 | 16.9 |
| 1985 | 651.7 | 0.59 | 0.41 | 0.15 | 0.09 | -125.5 | 769.2 | 16.3 |
| 1990 | 1,020.6 | 0.55 | 0.34 | 0.10 | 0.22 | -248.2 | 1,197.7 | 20.7 |
| 1993 | 1,616.9 | 0.71 | 0.35 | 0.18 | 0.03 | -68.8 | 1075. 0 | 6.4 |

*Sources*: Central Bank of Barbados, annual statistical digests, government estimates of revenue and expenditure.

**Figure 10.4**
**Domestic Debt Outstanding, December 1983**

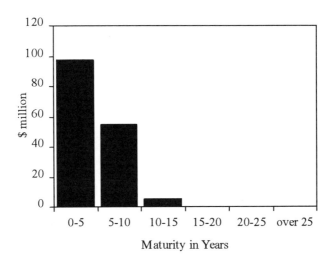

**Figure 10.5**
**Domestic Debt-Original Maturity, December 1993**

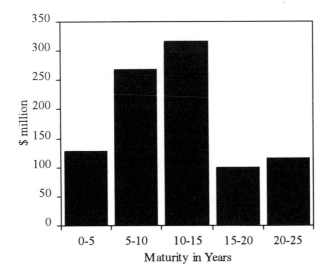

In contrast to the 1983 situation when there were no outstanding securities with original maturities of 0–5 years (see Figures 10.3), by 1993 this situation had changed dramatically. With the issuing of shorter-term treasury notes, maturities within the 0–5 year and 0–10 year period were now quite significant (see Figures 10.5 and 10.6). By 1994 following a special placement of nonmarket securities, the schedule of redemptions again showed maturities beyond the 20-year term, a scenario not evident since 1973. The result of the special issue was a more mixed basket of maturities as shown in Figure 10.7.

**Figure 10.6**
**Domestic Debt Outstanding, December 1993**

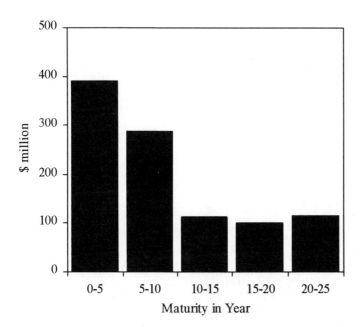

Yield curves on government securities tended to be upward sloping for most of the period, with the exception of 1981–1982 and 1992, when pressures of debt financing combined with tight bank liquidity to push short-term yields to levels in excess of longer maturities. However, inverted yield curves have been a temporary phenomenon from time to time and resulted

principally from high yields in treasury bills in tight money situations and
pressures on government financing. Yields tended to range between 7%
and 10% per annum, and given the relatively low levels of inflation real
returns tended to be positive with the exception of 1981–1982. As a result
there was no need for indexation of bonds as inflation rates tended to range
between 4% and 7%. For the same reason there was no pressure to issue
floating rate debt. This situation was possible not only because of low
inflation but also because of the fixed exchange rate of BDS$2 to US$1.
In this sense the Barbados case differs from most of Latin America in that
interest rates (both commercial bank interest rates and yields on securities)
had fallen since the peak period 1982–1983. Barbados was therefore able
to avoid the hyperinflation experiences of Latin America of the 1980s. This
was a distinction which it fought hard for international credit markets to
recognize so as to delink Barbados from what was familiarly known as the
Latin American debt crises of the 1980s.

**Figure 10.7**
**Barbados Domestic Debt-Annual Maturity**

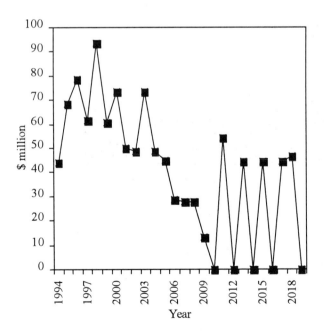

## DOMESTIC DEBT AND PRIVATE SECTOR CREDIT

In Barbados, controls tend to be placed on private sector credit but public sector credit proved more difficult to control, particularly in the pre-1994 period. About one-third of total bank credit financed the public sector in 1993 compared with 20% in 1983 and about 10% in 1973.

Barbados authorities abandoned credit controls in 1993 after almost 20 years of intermittent reliance on this instrument. In addition to high levels of reserve requirements, direct influence on treasury bill yields through the tender, limited open market operations, and direct interest rate controls were used to influence the relative cost of private sector credit and to indirectly influence the cost of government securities.

Virtually each increase in reserve requirements was accompanied by increases in interest rates. When interest rates were not sufficiently high to deter borrowers during periods of balance of payments difficulties, the likelihood of a reserve requirement response from the authorities was increased. Where reserve requirements were not used, the Central Bank attempted to bid up yields on treasury bills so as to encourage a shift into bills and out of credit. The objective was often less to discourage private sector credit (because levels of credit were not consistent with macroeconomic stability and foreign exchange sufficiency) than to shift the burden of financing of the government deficit away from the Central Bank and on to the private sector. As a result, when private sector debt was increasing too rapidly, domestic debt issues were increased to absorb liquidity either by way of secondary reserve requirements or interest rate manipulation.

## DOMESTIC DEBT AND CROWDING OUT

Rapid increases in domestic debt led from time to time to concerns about the crowding out of the private sector. However, attempts to reduce private sector credit by way of interest rate manipulation sometimes required excessively high rates of interest (14%–15%)—as was the case in the period 1981–1982. For Barbados these were high rates though they contrasted with Jamaica where interest rates at times rose as high as 30%, though complicated by considerations of exchange rate concerns and a campaign against capital flight. In Barbados, except for the 1981–1983 period, which was complicated by high international interest rates, yields on domestic securities were generally low and hardly ever exceeded 10%. With the notional freeing up of the banking system from interest rate controls and credit controls in 1993 there was likely to be increasing dependence on the government securities market to dampen private sector demand by way of increased yields on government securities. If the supply of funding via greater financing provoked increased government spending, then the axiom that funding will be spent by government as long as it is made available, often proved to be uncomfortably accurate.


## CENTRAL BANK INTERVENTION

Central Bank interventions in the market took several forms. Firstly, the Central Bank intervened to bring treasury bill rates down but was not able to bid them up so as to avoid holding an unnecessarily high level of treasury bills.

Secondly, the Central Bank also engaged in limited open market operations. This led to a dual role for the Central Bank—influencing yields at the primary level and providing liquidity at the secondary level. When increasing credit demand prompts commercial banks to unload treasury bills, yields ought to fall. However, because the Bank did not wish to hold government securities it would try to keep yields up. Market indicators and central bank objectives therefore exerted different influences on the treasury bill rate. For this reason some central banks are not involved at the stage of primary issues. However, in the Barbados, case because of the limited size of the market, development of independent primary buyers, as occurs in other developed countries was more of a challenge. Historically, central banks in developing countries have preferred to assume the role of residual financier—taking up shortfalls at tender.[7]

Open market operations in the discretionary sense were not conducted but prearranged margins were added on the buying side and deducted on the selling side for treasury bill purchases and sales. In early 1983 discretionary margins were more widely used, though an outside limit remained, so that full open market operations could not be said to have existed during the period. In 1999, as the Central Bank became the Central Securities Depository for securities under a dematerialized trading system, the Bank was poised to begin to conduct open-market operations using an automated platform, using the software of the Securities Exchange of Barbados.

## DOMESTIC DEBT AND THE INTEREST RATE STRUCTURE

Yields on government securities fluctuated according to government financing needs. Where government's financing needs were low, coupons on government securities and yields on treasury bills tended to be below the average lending rate, and tended to rise sharply in times of excessive government spending.

In especially illiquid situations, yields on government bonds have exceeded the ceiling on the average lending rate as government attempted to compete with commercial banks for surplus loanable funds. However, since commercial banks were the major investors in government securities, and they invest in excess of stipulated secondary reserve requirements, the investment of these surpluses constitute an income advantage to commercial banks during periods of excess liquidity. However, for the greater part of the period under study, yields on government securities tended to be below average lending rates.

Comparisons between rates of return on government securities became more important as securities requirements were increasingly used. While treasury bill yields tended to be higher than government bond yields, they were generally lower than banks' average lending rates and this had adverse implications for profitability to the extent that these securities were held in satisfaction of required secondary reserve requirements. They therefore became an inflexible part of banks' portfolios and represented an opportunity cost for banks.

The relationship between yields on government securities and interest rates offered and charged by commercial banks affected both deposit rate accumulation and shifts in investments by banks between public and private sector. Yields on government securities were usually higher that the minimum savings rate. A small differential was sufficient to satisfy the depositor that the additional liquidity, convenience and accessibility of depositing with commercial banks exceeded the differential in favor of government securities. In Barbados during the period 1973–1993 yields on treasury bills generally tended to exceed average deposit rates (1975, 1985 and 1989 were exceptions). To that extent interest rates offered on government securities were not likely to attract depositors to withdraw funds from commercial banks thus creating liquidity problems.

Conversely, in 1989 when deposit growth was stagnant, treasury bill yields at levels higher than minimum deposit rates would have added to the competitive environment. Deposit rates were therefore raised to attract deposit growth and the ceiling on lending rates increased to dampen private sector demand. Generally, securities in the Caribbean tended to be more illiquid than similar investments in developed markets. In the Barbados case, yields on government securities did not exceed long-term deposit rates by a sufficiently wide margin as to exceed the perceived transactions cost, inconvenience and the cost of illiquidity of investing in government securities.

## LIQUIDITY AND NEW DOMESTIC ISSUES

Liquidity shortages were as challenging as periods of excess liquidity. While preoccupation with the financing of government deficit tended to lead to a focus on new issues of government debt, net increases in government debt were only one aspect of the burden of financing. Significant reductions in excess liquidity of commercial banks prompted the sale of securities by banks to the Central Bank, thus leading to increased holding of government securities by the bank even during periods of controlled government spending. This was the case during periods of liquidity shortages.

However, liquidity shortages and fiscal deficits gave way in the mid-1990s to situations of excess liquidity accompanied by small fiscal deficits, creating unusual pressures for investment instruments and a demand for securities in an environment where government was not in need of financing. Nevertheless, efforts were made to provide avenues for investment in order to preempt capital flight driven by a desire for return on assets.

This phenomenon created an interest cost for government but had the advantage of preventing an outflow of foreign exchange. The extent to which this situation could be ignored depended on the level of international interest rates vis-à-vis local rates. Where international rates are low relative to domestic rates the pressure of capital flight is diminished. However, where rates are higher than domestic rates the pressure to find avenues of investment tends to increase. Where, however, international rates are substantially higher than local rates, the issue of local securities is less likely to solve the problem. Fortunately, during the late 1990s, the period when this phenomenon was evident, international rates were lower than domestic rates, thus facilitating a domestic solution to excess liquidity situations.

## LIQUIDITY DEBT MANAGEMENT AND THE GOVERNMENT SECURITIES MARKET

Generally, however because of the underdeveloped state of the stock market in Barbados, the substitution between bonds and money is relatively low.     The periodically high level of credit to Government by way of overdraft facilities was a reflection both of its dependence on short-term credit and the underdeveloped state of capital markets. Normally, there is less incentive for a movement out of deposits into bonds following increases in reserve requirements even if treasury bill rates rise, because of lack of liquidity in the market. The illiquidity of issues affects commercial banks less as they were able to buy and sell treasury bills to the Central Bank but nonbanks and individuals were affected to an even greater extent by the lack of depth in the market. Since banks already have this facility and they already form the small core of brokers and dealers in the securities market, the incentive for entering the market as active market-makers was therefore reduced. As a result, there was little activity in the market in secondary securities and though government securities may be listed and traded on the Securities Exchange, as there were no brokers with sufficient capital to buy and sell these securities, they in reality seldom traded.

The Central Bank's open market operations are very limited and not truly influenced by market forces. In periods of credit controls and interest rate controls situations of reductions in bank liquidity and increased credit demand were handled by authorities by reducing credit to the foreign exchange-using sectors or by raising interest rates. In the increasingly liberalized environment of the late 1990s and more especially in the twenty-first century, these options will become less available so that greater reliance is likely to be placed on the securities market and on the responses of investors to yields on government securities. A consequence of this is that authorities will be less able to keep interest rates down as a means of combating inflation and of controlling operational costs of the business sector.

The trend toward a liberalized environment will require a well functioning securities market in the twenty-first century. A well-developed capital market will require full information for efficient functioning if prices are to reflect market values. It will also require adequate capitalization by brokers if they are to give depth to the market.

## SECONDARY RESERVE REQUIREMENTS IN THE REACTION FUNCTION FOR POLICY MAKING AND THE IMPACT ON THE BALANCE OF PAYMENTS

Changes in liquidity were frequently policy induced. Indeed primary and secondary reserve requirements were a critical part of the process of influencing the level of credit in the Caribbean whether such shocks were money-induced or credit induced, and the transmission process through the banking system was rapid and efficient and prompted secondary costs, profit and portfolio planning adjustments by commercial banks, many of which reinforced the initial volume adjustment, and impacted the monetary base. Emphasis on securities requirements is in fact a characteristic of countries with incomplete markets as is the case in almost all countries in the Caribbean including Barbados.

### Secondary Reserve Requirements and Domestic Debt

Commercial banks' secondary reserve requirements were a significant factor in government financing and a major characteristic of most Caribbean economies. Barbados was no exception. The case of Barbados between 1973 and 1991 vividly illustrates the reserve requirement response of authorities to changes in the balance on external account. The rapid rise in domestic debt was made possible largely as a result of increased reserve requirements. In response to balance of payments difficulties reserves were raised from 3% of deposits in 1973 in a series of movements to 20% by 1978. Almost each year coincided with years of deficits in the balance on external account. As the balance of payments drifted into deficit in 1980, reserve requirements were again raised by five percentage points to 27% of deposits. They remained there until 1986 when the securities component, mostly treasury bills, was increased by three percentage points until 1991 following two years of successive balance of payments deficits (see Table 10.5). While reserve requirements provided government with a captive market for securities it carried the disadvantage of removing pressures for fiscal discipline.

It has been argued that securities requirements are a fiscal rather than a monetary tool. It is not clear that the propensity to import of government is lower than that of the private sector or that the impact on the balance of payments of government spending differs from that of the private sector. Evidence is therefore inconclusive on whether the effectiveness of this policy is due to the crowding out effect or to a possibly lower impact on the balance of payments from government expenditures.

**Table 10.5**

**Treasury Bill Issues, Redemptions and Average Tender Rate, 1974–1993**

**$ million**

| Period | Issued | Redeemed | Outstanding at calendar year-end | Average tender rate at calendar year-end (%) |
|--------|--------|----------|----------------------------------|----------------------------------------------|
| 1974 | 131.4 | 111.6 | 47.0 | 8.04 |
| 1975 | 227.7 | 208.3 | 56.9 | 4.00 |
| 1976 | 345.3 | 305.2 | 94.6 | 4.50 |
| 1977 | 411.6 | 397.4 | 114.4 | 5.00 |
| 1978 | 429.0 | 427.3 | 132.1 | 4.79 |
| 1979 | 478.9 | 461.3 | 149.4 | 4.95 |
| 1980 | 555.5 | 535.6 | 164.2 | 6.19 |
| 1981 | 817.2 | 746.4 | 228.1 | 13.82 |
| 1982 | 944.7 | 913.0 | 265.6 | 11.34 |
| 1983 | 955.3 | 918.1 | 302.3 | 6.81 |
| 1984 | 1,058.0 | 998.9 | 350.6 | 7.19 |
| 1985 | 1,232.0 | 1170.3 | 405.0 | 4.58 |
| 1986 | 1,353.0 | 1344.9 | 422.5 | 4.34 |
| 1987 | 1,482.0 | 1491.7 | 423.9 | 4.99 |
| 1988 | 1,373.0 | 1369.6 | 44.0 | 4.71 |
| 1989 | 1,393.0 | 1396.4 | 427.0 | 5.82 |
| 1990 | 1,509.0 | 1412.2 | 506.2 | 8.06 |
| 1991 | 1,619.0 | 1642.9 | 497.8 | 11.30 |
| 1992 | 1,987.0 | 1857.9 | 635.2 | 6.60 |
| 1993 | 2,662.0 | 2695.3 | 648.5 | 7.23 |

*Sources*: Central Bank of Barbados, annual statistical digests.

Reliance on secondary reserve requirements was largely influenced by the thin market in securities. Had the facility existed for the public to liquidate short-term debt at short notice it would have been possible to encourage the holding of government issues without resorting to forced subscription by way of reserve requirements.

Like the growth of domestic debt, increases in reserve requirements tended to be mostly one way. In Barbados securities requirements proved difficult to reverse. Secondary reserve requirements rose steadily over the 20 years prior to 1991 when the required securities ratio was reduced by two percentage points. This contrasted with Trinidad and Tobago and Jamaica, where authorities raised and at other times lowered liquid assets ratios. These countries differed, however, from Barbados in the greater variety of instruments available to the public and greater depth in the securities market.

The following analysis examines the variables in the reaction function which prompted the use of reserve and securities requirements—required holdings of government securities—as a monetary policy tool. It analyzes their impact on the adjustment processes and on the outturn for the balance of payments. Monetary tools are not always used sequentially but in collaboration with other controls so that it is frequently not possible to conclude over short periods that the objectives achieved can be attributed solely to any one policy tool. While it can be claimed that the use of required securities requirements is a monetary tool, it is included here insofar as these securities are government securities and their issue has implications for the use of fiscal policy as a tool of balance of payments management as well.

By examining the reaction function of authorities over a 20-year period 1971–1991 (a period of significant changes in these statutory requirements) it is possible to evaluate the significance of this tool in the process of balance of payments correction. A linear dynamic reaction function for reserve requirements is applied, which has as its independent variables, the balance of payments, credit, output, prices, the money supply, interest rates and the fiscal deficit. This is expressed in the function:

$$Rq = b_0 + b_1 FX_{(t-1)} + b_2 Cr_{(t-1)} + b_3 Y + b_4 P + b_5 Ms + b_6 I + b_7 D_{(t-1)} + u$$

where

Rq = reserve requirements
FX = balance on external account
Cr = commercial bank credit net of government
Y  = GDP
P  = prices
Ms = money supply
I  = interest rates
D  = fiscal deficit
u  = error term

It is assumed that governments attempt to maximize some welfare function subject to balance in the external accounts, a controllable fiscal deficit, reasonable access to private sector credit and some level of inflation. This is a relatively standard approach to maximizing a welfare function. Welfare is measured by real GDP in the absence of any other meaningful measure. The overall balance on external account is used here rather than the current account balance since foreign capital flows into Barbados are an important means of achieving balance in the external account even in normal times and are not merely a balancing item.

Most of the econometric work performing such tests in developed countries identify interest rates or credit as the dependent variable. The limited emphasis on government securities requirements is explained by their limited use in developed countries where open market operations are more evident, but in developing countries where open market operations are not fully functional this technique is heavily relied upon.

The use of the reserve and securities requirement as a policy tool is illustrated by the period 1973–1980. In response to balance of payments difficulties, the level of required reserves was raised from 3% in 1973 to 20% in 1978 and in 1980 by seven percentage points to 27% of deposits. They remained there until 1986 when the securities component was increased by three percentage points. Further increases were evident in 1991.

Before examining the results of the OLS equations, a brief assessment of rationale for selection of the explanatory variables in the reaction function of authorities is offered.

In the regression equation the external account balance is lagged one period in initial test runs. It is expected that the external account is the single most critical variable explaining the use of reserve and securities requirements. Foreign exchange reserves are used as a proxy for the balance of payments, mirroring their use by authorities. The evidence is that authorities observe trends in the level of foreign exchange reserves on a current basis and respond according to the timing and seasonalities of these flows.

The relationship between economic growth and changes in reserve requirements suggests that if economic growth exceeds a level consistent with a sustainable foreign exchange reserves, the balance of payments deteriorates. Also short-term balance of payments problems are often corrected by suppressing demand and hence output. When the required response time is very short, reserve or securities requirements tend to be the preferred option. Prior period output is entered in the initial equation in recognition of this lagged response.

The third independent variable used in the regression equation is credit to the private sector by commercial banks. Credit enters through its response to other policy measures. Where credit limits are having the desired effect, for example, authorities may not attempt to impose reserve requirements particularly where the required adjustment is not substantial. If the desired adjustment is extensive both direct credit limits and reserve and securities requirements may be applied. The credit variable enters the OLS equation with the same time period as the dependent variable in initial test runs.

Money supply is included in the equation as an explanatory variable since the relationship between credit and the money supply is not symmetrical in time. Moreover, international financial institutions have increasingly used the monetary base as a crucial variable in the determination of monetary policy. If, however, money is an endogenous variable as claimed by some Caribbean economists it should not carry a very high weight in the results.

The transfer of credit from the private to the public sector crowds out the private sector but often protects the balance of payments from the deterioration that would otherwise have arisen from a money-financed deficit or from the undiverted additional private sector credit.

## Results

Several test runs were done using the initial basic equation. The reaction function was highly explanatory with an $R^2$ of 0.99. It was found that authorities responded to the explanatory variables with some lag. The results show a very strong relationship between the fiscal deficit and the authorities' decision to use reserve requirements and results were significant at the 5% level. Credit and the money supply were less significant and prices were not found to be important. The interest rate coefficient was not significant and was removed from the equation. The low t-value might be explained by the attempt by authorities to keep interest rates low, rendering them a poor indicator of demand pressures in the loan market. Changes in output were not significant to the reserve requirement decision. The sign of the output coefficient suggests that reserve and securities requirements were more likely to be used when growth in the economy was sluggish. As expected the balance of payments was the single most important explanatory variable and such decisions were taken on the basis of the current period balance of payments situation. Data revealed that changes in reserve requirements were large and discrete. This was evident in the high standard deviations despite a very high $R^2$. Alternative nonlinear specifications did not add to the rigor of the analysis.

The Durbin-Watson statistic at 2.01 did not suggest the presence of serial correlation of the residuals. This was confirmed by the Smith Orcutt test which did not reveal auto correlation of the residuals. Details of the equation which best explained the Barbados reserve requirement decision are given in Table 10.6

### Implications for the Balance of Payments

The results of regression analysis strongly suggest that the critical variables in the reaction function of authorities for the primary and secondary reserve decision are principally, the balance of payments, the fiscal deficit and, less so, output and the money supply. The transmission mechanism through commercial banks produces further credit reductions through cost and interest rate responses but result in cost-driven modifications to commercial bank behavior. To this extent the impact on the balance of payments is indirect and achieved through a reduction in credit and hence in spending. There is a direct effect on the balance of payments to the extent that banks may borrow temporarily from abroad.

## INTRA-REGIONAL DEBT MANAGEMENT IN THE 1980s

The management of intra-regional debt between Barbados and other Caribbean countries and to a limited extent between Caribbean and Latin American countries tends to be underemphasized. While the story of extraregional debt is well known, it is less well known that some regional economies were significant debtors to each other and that much of that debt was underperforming in the 1980s. In addition, comparisons with Latin American approaches to integration of debt suggest useful lessons for the management of regional debt.

**Table 10.6**
**Results of Regression: Reserve Requirements**

| Variable | Coefficient |
|---|---|
| constant | -39.97 |
| | (-1.39) |
| Fx | -0.137 |
| | (-2.63) |
| cr(-1) | 0.31 |
| | (-0.035) |
| Y | -0.056 |
| | (-0.073) |
| Ms | 0.345 |
| | (-0.073) |
| Def(-1) | -0.205 |
| | (-4.69) |
| R2 | 0.997 |
| D.W | 2.01 |
| SEE | 10.2 |
| Log likelihood | -63.7 |
| F statistic | 886.95 |

(t-statistics are in parentheses)

During the beginning of the 1980s the view was that developing countries could grow their way out of their debt service difficulties. This did not occur. By 1987 it was clear that economic growth in the region was not sufficient to provide any significant relief in terms of debt service obligations. In addition intra-regional trade declined dramatically from the peak levels of 1983 in many Caribbean countries, and exports, though showing some improvement, continued to underperform in the late 1980s. The rationing of foreign exchange practiced in the region helped to slow the rate of growth of external debt but only at the expense of import contraction. Regional trade suffered as a result.

Despite the difficulties of Barbados in the 1980s, they were not sufficiently severe as to lead to rescheduling, refinancing, renegotiation of debt relief, debt-for-debt swaps, debt-for-equity swaps and countertrade arrangements, techniques which were common in Latin America during that period. This was partly because much of Caribbean debt was owed to governments and multilateral agencies and less to private banks who tended to be the entities more likely to use innovative techniques. Intra-regional debt was mostly negotiated at fixed rather than floating rates. In this way attempts by creditor countries to compensate themselves by forcing higher debt service burdens on debtor countries were avoided.

While the regional payments and settlement arrangement, the Caribbean Multilateral Clearing Facility (CMCF), was not specifically a debt arrangement but rather a payment arrangement, it was felt that by effecting settlement of current transactions without the use of hard currency, that regional governments would be able to keep the levels of regional debt to a minimum while at the same time economizing on the use of hard currency. The arrangement was itself not a product of the 1980s, having started in 1969 as an intra-regional payment scheme. It expanded and by 1976 had become an arrangement that offered credit to participants. The system permitted one country owed by another country to use that balance due to it to purchase goods and services from a third country without effecting settlement.

The facility reached its agreed limits in 1983 but lacked a medium-term window such as FOCEM the Latin American equivalent (Central American Monetary Stabilization Fund) which could provide extended credit. FOCEM, a medium-term facility provided one-year, five-year and eight-year loans and would have been a critical support mechanism. By the time Caribbean countries began examining the possibility of a window for providing long-term credit, most countries in the region were already experiencing balance of payments difficulties and could not find sufficient resources to start such a fund, nor were the possibilities of joining FOCEM a feasible option since the Caribbean would have been bringing very little to the fund and would not have been a contributor to the initial building up of that fund. While the opportunity for regional payment systems still existed, the experience of the 1980s suggested that credit lines on a multilateral basis might have proved difficult to implement.

The region's experience with bilateral lending was more promising. Government agencies and central banks in the region routinely bought into bond issues of regional governments. While these tended sometimes to be rolled over, the history of repayment tended to be much better than that for multilateral debt. Formal renegotiations were not the norm and sometimes nonpayment inadvertently led to a lengthening of maturities. Regional loans were never called.

Intra-regional public debt as a percentage of total public debt for 1980 and 1987 can be seen in Table 10.7

**Table 10.7**
**Intra-Regional Debt as Percentage of Total Debt**

| Country | 1980 | 1987 |
| --- | --- | --- |
| Bahamas | 4.72 | 9.48 |
| Barbados | 21.51 | 13.87 |
| Guyana | 11.88 | 18.25 |
| Jamaica | 13.37 | 12.27 |
| Trinidad and Tobago | 0.13 | 0.1 |

*Sources*: Various annual reports and trade reports of CARICOM Countries.

There were at least two such formal renegotiations by Barbados at the regional level. One, a debt owed by Barbados on the Trinidad market and the other, a debt owed principally by Guyana to creditors of the CMCF. In the first case the debt—a bond issue—was repaid and a direct loan obtained from the Central Bank of Trinidad and Tobago. In that case Barbados was the debtor. In the second case, Barbados was a creditor, and it involved CMCF debt totaling US$100 million, which was rescheduled by regional creditors of which Barbados was a significant creditor. The renegotiated terms offered a 10-year moratorium with final repayment over 20 years. Capitalization of interest payment by creditors is usually part of these arrangements, and this was the case of the CMCF rescheduling.

The refinancing method was used by Barbados only in informal arrangements, mostly in the case of credit extended by central banks in the region. In such cases there was no loan agreement and requests for refinancing or rollover of existing debt was usually accommodated without fanfare. This source of short-term financing in some cases extended over several years and was an important cushion for the Central Bank in the 1980s.

Barbados was a beneficiary of debt write offs by United States Agency for International Development (USAID) as part of a policy of the United States Government in the Caribbean. However, it also preceded the closure of the USAID office in Barbados and marked the effective end of USAID lending to Barbados.

While Barbados has never written off any debt due to other Caribbean countries, in 1998 central banks in the region pledged support to the initiative for highly indebted poor countries (HIPC), an initiative to write down debt of the more heavily indebted poor countries—in this case Guyana. Barbados never engaged in debt for equity arrangements in any CARICOM country, though consideration was given to doing so in the Guyana case but was complicated by the multilateral nature of the CMCF debt.

Even at the turn of the century the view still prevails in some circles that the establishment of an intra-regional support fund that is capitalized by participating countries could be helpful in pooling regional resources to provide a cushion in the event that member countries need critical balance of payments assistance or where bridging finance is necessary. It could prove an alternative to IMF financing in cases here the level of required adjustment and funding is not significant.

## FOREIGN BORROWING

Increasingly, fiscal deficits required the negotiation of foreign debt. Since its first significant foreign borrowing in 1959 for the financing of the Deep Water Harbor, Barbados continued to access foreign sources intermittently during the 1960s and early 1970s through project loans from friendly governments, mostly Canada, and from organizations such as CIDA, USAID, the World Bank, IADB, Crown Agents and similar agencies.

With the establishment of the Central Bank in 1972, much of the responsibility for sourcing foreign market borrowings was placed on accessing foreign borrowing for balance of payments support and for funding of development projects. Examples were private placements in the United Kingdom and Japanese markets (see Table 10.8).

There was a decided shift in emphasis on the holding of domestic versus foreign debt during the 20-year period 1973–1993. Up to the mid-1970s, prior to the establishment of the Central Bank and the discontinuance of the currency board system, the negotiation of foreign debt tended to be tied to projects; though the balance of payments benefitted from these borrowings they were not balance of payments support loans by design. This situation changed in the 1970s and 1980s, when balance of payments support loans were actively sought and resulted in reduced reliance on domestic debt in the second half of the 1980s. The share of domestic debt in total debt fell by 33 percentage points from the peak of 84% in 1977 to 51% by 1988 and thereafter rose slowly. Despite the declining share, domestic debt in absolute terms continued to grow during this period at much the same pace so that the growth rate of overall debt did not decline. The emphasis on the negotiation of foreign debt was driven by foreign exchange imperatives rather than by fiscal requirements. Authorities saw domestic debt as supplying domestic financing requirements only, while foreign borrowing satisfied both a foreign exchange need as well as a fiscal requirement.

In the 1980s and 1990s public market borrowings through the issue of foreign debt denominated in U.S. dollars were issued as balance of payments support loans and as development financing. During the early 1990s government pursued a policy of issuing new foreign debt only in amounts roughly equivalent to maturing debt, while in the latter part of the 1990s government embarked on a policy of reducing its foreign debt service ratio.

By December 1994 Barbados had reached the point where it could obtain a credit rating from Moody's of Ba2. Its success in reducing its foreign debt service issues and reducing its debt service ratio by substantive margins, influenced the decision of Moody's to give Barbados an improved rating of Ba1. This improved rating helped significantly in marketing foreign-denominated issues.

**Table 10.8**

**Foreign Debt: Significant Government Borrowing, 1980s and 1990s**

**Marketing Borrowings/Private Placements**

| Source | | Amount | Repayment |
|---|---|---|---|
| | Can$ | | |
| 1980 | Trinidad Bond | TT$40.0 million | 1990 |
| 1981 | Orion Bank | US$30.0 million | 1985–88 |
| 1985 | Natwest | US$25.0 million | 1989–92 |
| 1985 | Yen Bond A | Yen 5.0 billion | 1990 |
| 1986 | Natwest | US$40.0 million | 1990–93 |
| 1986 | Yen Bond B | Yen 4.3 billion | 1991 |
| 1987 | Barclays | £27 million | 1991–94 |
| 1988 | Yen Bond C | Yen 5.0 billion | 1994–98 |
| 1990 | Samuel Montague | US$25.0 million | 1993–97 |
| 1990 | Barclays de Zoete Wedd | £30.0 million | 2015 |
| 1990 | Citibank | US$20.0 million | 1995–97 |
| 1992 | Natwest | US$12.0 million | 1994–96 |
| 1994 | Bankers Trust | US$20.0 million | 1997 |
| 1994 | Bankers Trust | US$30.0 million | 1999 |
| 1995 | Citibank | US$40.0 million | 2002–05 |
| 1999 | Citibank | US$75.0 million | 2005–09 |

*Note*: Several other smaller loans were advanced by agencies and private bankers during the period. The most significant loans of these were in 1984 of US$24.5 million (1998–2004) for development of the airport-west coast highway and US$13.0 million loan for Mobil Oil in 1983. Another significant initiative was a guarantee of a loan of US$40.6 million by Creditanstalt for construction of the Arawak Cement Project. CIDA also played a very important role in airport development finance during the 1970s. All foreign loans were approved by Parliament.

*Sources*: Various annual reports of the Central Bank of Barbados and government estimates of revenue and expenditure, various issues.

In April 2000 Barbados received an investment grade from Standard and Poor"s and was given a foreign sovereign credit rating of A-. Some weeks after Moody's also elevated Barbados to investment grade, giving the country a rating of Baa2. These improved ratings permitted Barbados to successfully access the foreign markets at competitive rates.

On the regional front, the government utilized the regional market, mostly the Trinidad market, on three occasions. First it obtained a loan of $20 million on the Trinidad and Tobago market in 1977 and refinanced this with a U.S. dollar bond in 1983. Another regional bond was financed mostly by Trinidad and Tobago subscribers in 1994. Again in 1999, a bond of US$75 million was successfully floated in the regional market. These issues were made possible because of the pool of U.S. dollars that had become more available on the regional market for investment in medium- and long-term securities. In addition, since potential investors are more in tune with the credit worthiness of Caribbean countries, the marketing of such issues regionally became relatively simple. Such regional issues had the added advantage of assisting in the development of a regional securities market and in the development of the stock exchanges of the region.

## SUMMARY AND CONCLUSION

Management of the public debt was modified according to domestic economic circumstances and to changes in the international environment. Toward the end of the century as Barbados' credit rating improved and it became an investment grade borrower, significantly wider opportunities were made available. However, borrowing was seen as a means of achieving both domestic stabilization and, from time to time, foreign exchange adequacy. However, early borrowings for balance of payments support in the 1980s and early 1990s were completely different from later borrowings. The latter borrowings built confidence and demonstrated the strength of the economy rather than its weakness. At the domestic level, government's debt management strategy continued throughout the period to marry financing needs with liquidity management, but needed to constantly be sensitive to private sector borrowing requirements.

### NOTES

1. Future interest payments will simply be transfer payments from taxpayer to bond holder. The bond holders are the commercial banks—who pass on interest charges—the national insurance and the savings bank.

2.  The term stabilization does not specifically refer to programs with international financial institutions, but where there exited at the time include periods when such programs were in place.

3.  Government borrowed on the United Kingdom and Japanese markets during the period.

4.  The Local Loans act provides authority for the issue of government debenture and treasury notes and the treasury bill and Tax Reserve Certificate act provides authority for the issue of treasury bills. Advances from the Central Bank are limited to 10% of current revenue but was raised to 17.5% of current revenue during the period 1981–1994. This is controlled by the Administration and Audit Act.

5. These securities were issued specifically to the Barbados National Bank as government fulfilled a guarantee of nonperforming loans with that bank.

6. Issues of savings bonds were limited to $50 million per year by administrative direction.

7. There is no legal limit to the Central Bank holdings of government securities but there is an administrative limit set internally by the Bank.  However, it applies to primary issues and not purchases on the secondary market.

# 11

## Incentives for Economic Development

### INTRODUCTION

While incentives were not always explicitly taken into account in developing budgets, tax incentives have important implications for revenues, mostly in terms of revenue forgone, but do not fall easily into an analysis of tax receipts. They imply acceptance of short-term revenue losses against expectation of long-term gains and a projection that a potentially greater scale of activities can be attained in the long term. Other potential gains include improvement in the skills base and exposure of a wider percentage of the population to business and to entrepreneurial activity. Policies on tax incentives are evaluated against this background.

Tax incentives were sometimes costed in the year in which they were introduced, but their impact on the budget was not estimated on a continuing basis. Incentives were given to certain sectors and to activities which were thought to be critical to the economic development of the country, mostly in the manufacturing sector.

The infant industry argument was often offered as a need for a temporary subsidy, but the general practice was for tariffs to remain in place long after they had been introduced. In choosing what incentives to offer, selection was often based on factors such as capital/labor ratios, import substitution benefits or foreign exchange needs and domestic value added. In addition, it was often necessary to weigh short-run against long-run benefits and to take into account possible pre-emptive action by the taxpayer.

Such investment incentives took various forms including accelerated depreciation and investment credits. Investment incentives were generally used to direct capital to tax-favored industries.

## TAX INCENTIVES TO MANUFACTURING

Tax incentives to the manufacturing sector were part of the facilitatory approach to developing an industrial sector. Barbados decided in the early 1970s to accelerate the pace of industrial development through the "industrialization by invitation approach." This was evidenced in the passing of the Fiscal Incentives Act in 1974, and occurred in the context of the Treaty of Chaguaramas and the Harmonization of CARICOM Trade Development efforts. Companies exporting outside of CARICOM were offered a 10-year tax holiday, and countries exporting within the Caribbean were given exemptions for 6 to 10 years. This varied depending on the local value added contribution of the project. Raw materials imported for use in production were given tax-free status. Other facilities included factory accommodation at industrial estates set up for housing these activities and for many years (until 1992) only nominal rents were imposed. At the end of the tax holiday, some concessions were still available. Exporters who shipped goods to countries outside CARICOM were allowed a tax rebate of up to 80.5%. In addition, from the mid-1970s export guarantee schemes, pre- and post-shipment finance and small business guarantee schemes were provided through the Central Bank. Also, up to 1992 special rediscount schemes were available through the Central Bank to finance working capital where banks were experiencing liquidity shortages.

During the early 1990s an export rebate was introduced whereby an exporter who shipped a maximum of 93% of exports outside CARICOM was able to reduce his effective rate of tax to 2.6%. Manufacturing and exporting companies that benefit from incentives were allowed to remit dividends abroad without incurring the 15% tax, where they were not being taxed in the country to which they were remitted. Where they were subject to a tax in the country to which they were remitted, they were required to pay a withholding tax in Barbados—at the lower of the Barbados and foreign rates.

## TAX INCENTIVES TO THE INTERNATIONAL BUSINESS SECTOR

Acceleration of the pace of development of the international business and financial services sectors was part of a strategy which started in 1970s and was intended to widen the country's economic base, to attract additional revenues, to bolster foreign exchange and to enhance employment possibilities.

The term "the international business sector" was used to refer to the activities of foreign-owned and foreign-controlled companies set up under special legislation. This legislation offered tax concessions or exempted these companies from corporate and other taxes altogether, provided they did business "from within" Barbados and not "in" Barbados. These "offshore" companies were not necessarily in the business of finance, but since the main activities that were transacted through Barbados tended to be their financial activities, the subsector and the companies that provide support services to them are referred to as the international financial services sector or more frequently as the international business sector.

As early as 1965 Barbados made its first attempts to encourage foreign companies to domicile their companies in Barbados through the offer of very attractive tax incentives, but the sector was not given much attention until the mid-1970s. These entities included international business companies, captive insurance companies, foreign sales corporations, offshore banks, trusts, limited liability companies and ship registrants.

The first piece of legislation was the International Business Companies Act and was passed in 1965. It was followed by Captive Insurance Legislation in 1983, the Foreign Sales Corporation Act in 1984 and the Offshore Banking Act in 1985. International trusts and Societies with Restricted Liability (SRLs) came much later, in 1995. Shipping legislation was also enacted much earlier but was not given much attention until the 1980s. At December 1999 the number of these entities registered had grown considerably compared with over 20 years earlier.

The most significant growth was in the number of international business companies and the number of foreign sales corporations. Growth of captive insurance business floundered in the late 1980s when Barbados lost the exemption from US federal excise tax, and grew more slowly thereafter.

## GOVERNMENT POLICY AND THE INTERNATIONAL BUSINESS SERVICES SECTOR

Tax-sparing legislation was the main technique used by government to attract these companies but it was supplemented by a series of double taxation treaties that improved the tax advantage by offering tax offset opportunities. Most of the treaty negotiations were concluded in the 1980s but others were added in the 1990s. These further enhanced Barbados' attractiveness as a domicile in which to do business.[1]

At the international level, the most-favored nation clause in the General Agreement on Trade in Services (GATS) to which Barbados had signed on and to which it had given specific commitments, made it imperative that Barbados clarify the strategic direction in which it will move with regard to further bilateral treaty negotiations given the existence of the Most Favored Nation (MFN) clause in GATS, which requires countries to offer to others benefits offered to the most favored.

Barbados commitment to ensuring that the domicile remains one of the highest repute and of the highest integrity, is demonstrated in its association with entities and organizations which promote such objectives. Barbados was among the countries to sign the Tax Information Exchange Agreement with United States, and was among the initiators of the Caribbean Financial Action Task Force on money laundering.

Nevertheless, challenges to this and other similar domiciles continue. These continued challenges to the domicile from the IRS in some jurisdictions may explain the lack of enthusiasm for committing to significant investment in training in some of these areas, for example, financial management. However, professional organizations are encouraged to bring these skills on board through their own initiatives.

The contribution of the sector to the economy is primarily in the area of foreign exchange earnings and less so, tax revenue. The international financial services sector is not a major employer, nor is there much scope for employment of low-skilled workers. However, the demand for skills of the middle and upper-income groups is likely to continue and the diversity and depth of required skills is likely to increase, particularly if IRS in home countries continues to insist on "mind and management" residing in the domicile as a criteria for qualifying for tax concessions. The challenge is for government to identify the skills needed and to prepare its workforce.

### International Business Companies—Low Tax Regime

International business companies represent the largest category of offshore companies and span a wide range of activities. These companies are charged a rate of tax on profits ranging from 1% to 2.5%. They are also allowed exemption from import duty on articles for use in the business. Freedom from exchange controls and income tax concessions for expatriate employees resident in Barbados are further attractions for the investor.

This sector makes an important contribution to foreign exchange earnings. It provides employment opportunities both direct and indirect for skilled and unskilled workers, enhances the development and expansion of Barbados' information technology infrastructure and results in the growth of support industries through the purchase of goods and services.

According to a 1994 report on the sector, based on a survey of the sector through accounting firms, a contribution of $57 million in foreign exchange to the Barbados economy in 1993 could be identified. The report notes that on the assumption that the response represented no less than 75% and no more than 90% of the total contribution of the sector, a total earnings figure of between $65 million and $75 million is likely. Using the unit contribution per company in 1993, the contribution of the sector in 1997 could be approximately $100 million. Other unofficial estimates by accounting firms have suggested a figure in the region of $150 million. Strict balance of payments estimates from the official balance of payments survey, put the figure for 1999 at around $136 million. The contribution of the sector to foreign exchange earnings is through taxes, license fees and payroll and other costs. The 1993 survey indicates that the sector contributed $9.7 million in license fees. The contribution to payroll costs in the same year was $20.9 million.[2]

Within the last several years the sector has been seriously challenged by moves by individual governments in metropolitan countries to block companies that establish headquarters in these jurisdictions from benefitting from the exempt tax status that they derive from incorporating in Barbados.

Essentially, the question tends to hinge on the fine line between tax planning and tax avoidance.[3] The test case approach has often been used, though this failed in 1995. Generally speaking the old criteria of operating "from within" and not "within" as the basis for taxability have been called into question.

One possibility is that, companies' home countries may insist that a greater number of persons need to be employed in these operations as part of the process of satisfying revenue authorities at home of the "mind and management criteria." Even though this may be largely satisfied, the challenges are likely to continue.

During 1998 and more especially 1999, in response to international attacks against the tax incentives offered in the sector, there was an initiative to reduce or eliminate the distinction between the domestic and offshore sectors. Toward the end of the century, feasibility studies were being conducted on the tax and revenue and business impact of tax integration.

## The Exemption for Foreign Sales Corporation

A foreign sales corporation is a special type of U.S. corporation that export's outside of the United States but may register to do business in, and is therefore taxable in Barbados.[4] This vehicle is designed to stimulate U.S. exports through the benefit of a partial tax exemption on export income. These companies are managed by accounting firms or by independent managers. Early in 1999 the WTO Appelate Court ruled that US tax incentives favoring foreign sales corporations were a contravention of WTO regulations and were a prohibited export subsidy. A US congressional Committee subsequently took action to repeal the FSC provisions and to put in its place alternative provisions which gave companies tax breaks if they gave up the earlier incentives. It has been argued by the US that the new rule does not represent a subsidy and rather that it is of general application, and that it is not applied only to exporters. Indications were that WTO was still unhappy about the new US regulations. Barbados, Guam, the U.S. Virgin Islands, and a few other counties would be most affected by an unfavorable WTO ruling.

## Offshore Banks—Low Tax Regime

Offshore banks are generally set up to do the banking business of a large group of clients or a range of subsidiary companies. The establishment of offshore banks is monitored by the Central Bank of Barbados. Through this oversight, the country has managed to avoid unsavory exposure and has maintained its reputation as a high-quality offshore center. Over 85% of the assets of offshore banks are held by large international banks. These banks are from home country jurisdictions with reliable supervision and this has helped to ensure the integrity of the sector.

## Exempt Insurance Companies—Tax Exempt Captives

Exempt insurance (captive insurance) companies typically engage in self-insurance for themselves or their group and operate in a totally income-tax-free environment.[5] This sector continues to make steady advances, but has been subject to a number of challenges from other jurisdictions. One U.S. challenge was the possibility that the IRS would require that captive insurance companies needed to show that they were covering third-party risk. This fear did not, however, materialize.[6]

The sector continues to grow despite the challenges. Extension of the guarantee of benefits to this sector in 1995 from 15 to 30 years suggested that the Government was committed to continued encouragement of these entities. Other vehicles include Trusts, SRLs and Ship Registration.

Barbados' trust legislation permits easy establishment of a trust. This may be combined with existing financial legislation to offer settlers and beneficiaries considerable advantages in taxation and asset protection.[7] The development of safe and available vehicles for management through establishment of management companies, the use of local banks' trust companies or offshore banks are spin-offs of these trust vehicles.

An SRL (Society for Restricted Liability) is a group of two or more persons who carry on a stated business for a limited period, but is neither a partnership nor a corporation. It has a separate legal personality from the owners and all owners have limited liability. It can be formed as a pass-through entity for tax purposes. For this purpose it is a useful vehicle for tax planners and is likely to be used more in the future, particularly since a 1998 decision of the IRS in the United States appeared to sanction its use.

Legislation on shipping is the least well known of these vehicles. The Ship Registration Act was amended in 1994 and 1996. The last amendment facilitates registration and simultaneous incorporation for operating purposes.[8]

## TAX INCENTIVES TO THE INFORMATICS SECTOR,
### 1970s–1990s

Since the late 1970s the informatics subsector has been another area whose growth and development government has been encouraged through the use of tax incentives. The informatics subsector forms part of that subgroup of international business companies (IBCs) set up under this type of legislation but, unlike most other types of companies, a much greater part of the input into their operations takes place in Barbados and such activities are not confined to merely financial operations.

IBCs have significant physical presence in Barbados, but export their products overseas. This was facilitated by revision to the IBC Act in 1991, which permitted companies to manufacture and otherwise process locally and continue to benefit from IBC tax exemptions, provided they manufactured or processed for export to countries outside CARICOM.[9]

Despite setbacks in the information technology subsector in the late 1990s, this was an important source of employment for Barbados in the 1970s and 1980s. The sector, despite some challenges, continued to be an important sector for Barbados. The country's location, which places it in the same time zone as the eastern seaboard of the United States, its good telecommunications system, and its special low tax regime are major advantages. Another is the reduced cost of doing business, which is estimated at some 40% to 50% of doing business in United States, and Canada, while allowing companies to maintain quality. The contribution of this sector is evident in the purchase of local services. Of the $20.9 million in payroll costs contributed by IBCs and other offshore entities in 1993, a significant portion was attributed largely to the labor-intensive informatics industry.

The information technology subsector is funded primarily by foreign capital. Foreign companies are required to bring all required capital into Barbados as a condition of establishment under the international business company legislation. Hardware and software are allowed into the country free of duty, provided they are used for the specified purpose and continue in that use for at least a period of five years. However, given the pace of change in technology and the need to continually upgrade equipment, companies are not always able to retain equipment for as long as five years. Local companies who are operating under the Companies Act of Barbados and who are exporting 100% of their services, pay a rate of tax of as low as 2.6%.

The government invested considerable resources in the training of young people in information technology.[10] In addition, importation of personal computers by individuals was permitted into the country free of duty so as to encourage national familiarity with the technology.

Generally, the tax incentives granted to this sector were particularly helpful. However, the development of the sector needs to be integrated with the domestic sector so that information systems at the cutting edge of technology become a part of industrial development across all sectors.

The challenges facing the informatics sector as the country approaches the start of a new century relate to control of operational costs, utility costs, improved labor flexibility and the challenge of moving to the high end of the market. It is important that input costs in the sector are kept low. In addition, because of the monopoly nature of the telecommunications industry (Cable and Wireless) it is difficult to achieve sufficiently low levels of utility costs desirable for the sector's improved competitiveness. In addition, labor flexibility will be important if managers are to make on the spot decisions relating to work allocation and scheduling.

In the area of skills development, if Barbados is to be at the high end of the market, the extent of computer proficiency of students leaving secondary and tertiary institutions will need to be improved. However, educational levels remain relatively high and despite concerns about slippage in some areas, the capability to push the sector forward exists but requires nurturing.

## DEVELOPMENTS IN THE INTERNATIONAL FINANCIAL SECTOR IN 2000

Toward the end of the decade of the nineties there was a concerted attack on the jurisdictions like Barbados which were attempting to develop themselves as international financial centers. In 1998 the OECD published a report on Harmful Tax Competition. The report deemed the low tax and no tax jurisdictions (Barbados is low tax) to be harmful. As a consequence of this report an OECD forum was set up on harmful tax practices.

Almost simultaneously, a Financial Stability Forum (FSF) was set up by the Bank for International Settlements (BIS) in conjunction with other international institutions with a mandate to put measures in place to eliminate volatile capital flows. Three Committees were set up by the FSF, one of which was to examine Offshore Centers. While Barbados never marketed itself as an offshore center, it was included in the survey. A third initiative was launched to examine money laundering, this time by the Financial Action Task Force, a group of European countries, supplemented by a few international organizations.

These organizations issued reports in 2000 and listed certain countries in various categories, the Financial Stability Forum on May 26, 2000, the Financial Action Task Force on June 23, 2000 and the OECD on June 26, 2000. The Financial Stability's Report identified three groups of "offshore financial centers." It placed Barbados in Group 2, despite the fact that the Report noted that transactions out of these centers had posed no threat to financial stability. (Group 1 was deemed to be satisfactory, Group 2 was deemed to have the appropriate structures in place but in need of improvement and Group 3 to be in need of urgent remedial work.) Barbados was not happy with this, with neither the process, which was based on perception, nor the result which did not tally with its own evaluation of itself. It noted that contrary to what one would have expected based on knowledge of various jurisdictions, that no developing country had been cited in Group 1 and that Barbados had as much claim to being placed in Group 1 as some of those placed in that category. Barbados also argued the case of lack of jurisdiction by OECD and argued for an international organization to conduct such an evaluation.

The report of the Financial Action task force (also largely an OECD entity) did not cite Barbados as a jurisdiction in which money laundering was taking place. This result was expected since Barbados had been very careful to guard its good name and in order to keep out undesirable persons, had developed a screening process as well as linkages with both regional and international organizations to guard against such possibilities. Barbados had also assisted in the establishment of the Caribbean Financial Action Task Force (CFATF), a task force modeled on the European Financial Action Task Force (FATF). In addition to adopting the 30 ground rules of FATF, the CFATF had adopted another 19 guidelines for operation of its members. The country had opted for slow and sure growth rather than rapid and questionable growth. It could have grown possibly several times faster had it not been very selective. In addition Barbados had long adopted the Core Principles For Effective Bank Supervision which provide for the establishment of mechanisms for sharing information among supervisors. This too was known.

However, it was the OECD's list of tax havens, published on June 26, 2000 which caused most concern. First there was the question of jurisdiction. It was felt that international rules should be set by international bodies and not by special interest groups. In addition, it was the Barbados view that a country's tax system should be a matter of sovereign decision making. In the same way that other countries both developed and developing had given incentives to certain sectors and activities so as to encourage their growth, the same was done in Barbados to encourage the growth of the international business sector.

The designation of tax competition as "harmful" hit at the heart of the right of individual countries to put in place tax systems to encourage national economic development and growth, policies practiced for centuries by the same countries who would seek to prevent them in these small and young developing countries. In addition, the idea that tax competition is harmful runs against the trend espoused by most major developed countries who otherwise advocate that competition be encouraged and that capital be permitted to move globally, unfettered by national restrictions. Indeed developing countries worldwide are struggling to conform to these initiatives toward financial liberalization. One view was that the motive was revenue related and was in fact an anti-competitive move. Barbados was of the view that while it would take any action that was necessary to ensure that its jurisdiction was well run, it preferred that these matters be dealt with by international bodies, who had appropriate legal jurisdiction.

On June 26, 2000 Barbados was therefore named as a "tax haven." None of the countries which had signed a letter written to them by an OECD official in which they committed to eliminate "harmful tax practices" was named as "tax havens." This tended to highlight the fact that what was important was not transparent criteria relating to the reality of the integrity of the jurisdiction but, rather the signing of a letter of undertaking.

Over and above the question of jurisdiction the OECD criteria for determining a tax haven were thought to be less than transparent. One criterion which cited low or nominal taxes (either general or specific) implied that even where domestic and international taxes converged, that a generally low tax could lead to a country being classified as a tax haven. (The term "tax haven" is deemed to be pejorative.) A country could therefore have a single low tax applicable to both onshore and offshore activities and still not escape being listed as a tax haven. Another criterion was that a country could find itself on the list of tax havens if it was perceived by others as a place where residents of other countries could escape tax. It was the view of many small developing countries that the "perception" of others was a rather hazy and unscientific basis on which to evaluate a country, particularly if it was proposed that punitive action be taken on the basis of such "perceptions." Further, the definition of "offshore centers" classified centers as "offshore" if foreign transactions are substantially larger than domestic transactions. Yet, if small centers are to be successful in international business, foreign transactions must, by definition, be larger than domestic transactions. This effectively meant that irrespective of the adequacy of supervision, regulation or cooperation, small centers like Barbados could, despite complying in all respects, continue to be deemed "offshore," unless the criteria were modified. A new term seemed more palatable. This was desirable since it was noted that some larger metropolitan cities where the same relativities existed were not termed "offshore" centers. By the end of the century the issue was still developing. However, it was clear that at the beginning of the twenty-first century small size and powerlessness would be as great a disadvantage as it had been over the past 50 years.

**NOTES**

1. As of April 31, 1999 tax treaties existed with, among others, Canada, Finland, Norway, Sweden, Switzerland, United Kingdom, and CARICOM. Negotiations with Germany are proceeding and there are proposed talks with Japan and Brazil. Bilateral Investment treaties exist with Germany, Switzerland, United Kingdom, Venezuela, Cuba and Canada.

2. Other local costs include the purchase of professional services, communications, rents, travel, hospitality services and office services. The contribution of these costs amounted to $26 million in 1993, and represented the costs of employment, training, employee welfare contributions to health insurance and pension schemes.

3. Prior clarification would assist, but administrators are reluctant to directly approach revenue offices in the companies' home country to enquire what is permissible lest the whole package be called into question.

4. Companies pay an annual license fee in Barbados and this constitutes the Government's main source of direct revenue from these entities. Revenue from this source in 1997 is estimated at $23 million based on unit contribution in the 1993 survey.

5. Most recently, Revenue Canada challenged the legitimacy of certain types of foreign-accrued property income and deemed that passive income from certain sources such as captive insurance was taxable in Canada. This was the subject of efforts by local authorities to make such income exempt by treating exempt insurance companies in the same manner as domestic companies and invoking the foreign tax credit, to provide an eventual tax rate of 2.8% per annum.

6. The Tax Information Exchange Agreement (TIEA) to which Barbados is a signatory, renders Barbados a "foreign country" in which foreign sales corporation may incorporate and maintain an office under the provisions of the Foreign Sales Corporation Act 1984. Under the act, U.S. companies domiciled in Barbados may perform activities that generate income outside of U.S. possessions.

7. The trust funds may be managed under the Offshore Banking Act while IBCs may provide a mechanism to protect the confidentiality of trusts. The increasing number of volume of assets of high net worth individuals suggests that demand for this vehicle will intensify.

8. Barbados' attainment of ISO 9000 status, through the award of a certificate of approval as a ship registry, should enhance the possibilities for future business.

9. Most companies that fall into this category tend to operate in the informatics sector and most companies in the informatics subsector are IBCs. The sector is particularly labor intensive. In mid-1998, of the 47 companies operating in the sector, 25 are foreign-owned. The sector currently employs 2,972 persons, a reduced figure on three years ago. Foreign-owned information services accounts for 88.5% of employment in the sector.

10. Students are taught computer skills through the Barbados Community College, the Polytechnic, Erdiston Training College as well as schools at the University of the West Indies.

# 12

## Public Finance:  A Possible Approach for the Twenty-First Century

**INTRODUCTION**
This concluding chapter treats with the philosophical question of the future role of government relative to the private sector as facilitator, as provider of services, as equity holder and as regulator.   It attempts to draw conclusions about whether this role should be different for small countries than for large, and different for developing countries than for developed. It evaluates by reference to the performance of this small economy in the last 50 years, whether changes in the stance of governments were effective in achieving accelerated economic growth and macroeconomic stabilization. It extends many of the issues discussed here to small developing countries generally, and reflects on whether global initiatives that call for liberalization of markets, and smaller government are optimal for all countries.  Finally, it suggests  approaches that small countries might adopt in order to survive in the twenty-first century.

**PUBLIC EQUITY OWNERSHIP**
Since one of the major drawbacks to competitiveness in small countries is a small scale, it is logical to conclude that adequate equity capital in new projects can theoretically be accessed if potential investors pool their resources to provide large sums of capital.  This has not however, been achieved.  It was felt that the establishment of a stock exchange would have led to a greater effort to pool resources, so permitting large enterprises to develop and small enterprises to grow.  But the private sector's response

to the establishment of a stock exchange since 1987 has not led to this outcome.

The record shows that outside of the construction sector, except for a few isolated cases of large manufacturing operations, and a few large tourists establishments, many of which are foreign-owned, it has proved very difficult for the local private sector to launch large enterprises of any sort.

Government, on the other hand, can claim or was able to claim ownership or part ownership of several large commercial enterprises. Not only did government establish statutory boards to engage in developmental activity, but it took the lead in establishing industrial operations, both alone and in concert with other entities. In 1966 the government set up a milk-producing plant in cooperation with a New Zealand firm. This plant later launched into the production of juices, yogurts and ice cream.

In 1979 government, in cooperation with a Canadian firm, Maple Leaf of Canada, established a flour mill. This operation supplied flour to the local population and to the region for many years and remained a government majority-owned operation until 1992, when the government, in urgent need of foreign exchange, disposed of its shares. The Hilton Hotel was for many years an example of a successful operation initiated and owned by government. In 1999 it ceased operations temporarily to allow for its rebuilding, and is expected to continue to be a partly government-owned operation.

The Arawak Cement Plant established in 1981 is yet another example of a major industrial activity initiated by government. It was partly owned by the Government of Trinidad and Tobago. While its profitability was poor for many years, it survived in its initial form and structure until 1994, when it was sold to private sector owners in the wake of a call for privatization.

The ownership and operation of Heywoods Hotel was one of the government's last attempts in the twentieth century to initiate, own and operate an industrial company. The profitability record of this operation was poor and despite several efforts it did not attain profitability until it was sold to a private sector company in the mid-1990s.

Where government-owned commercial type enterprises fail, it tends to add to the view that such failures are typical and frequent, even when there may be more successes than failures, and more failures on a relative basis in the private sector than in the public sector. In some cases prolonged underperformance of state enterprises results from the absence of termination mechanisms, particularly in countries where capital markets are thin and the culture of private investment is embryonic—as in Barbados.

The government was also a significant shareholder in the main telecommunications company for many years. This was a very profitable undertaking despite public regulation by a Public Utilities Board. The government disposed of its shares in Cable and Wireless in 1991 when it was in dire need of foreign exchange. The agreement included a buyback arrangement that would allow it to repossess its shares within a five-year period. Government did not exercise its option at the end of the five-year period, and the monopoly situation proved very restrictive.

The point however, is that it tended to be the government rather than the private sector which was able to establish large commercial operations. However, charges of inefficiency in the 1980s and 1990s, and the urgent need for foreign exchange prompted several privatizations of some of these enterprises. However, there is a lesson to be learned from the experience of the government in establishing these enterprises. The error was, perhaps that government chose to operate these enterprises for too long a period.

It is, however, timely to reflect on whether small countries like Barbados should allow the rhetoric of the international financial institutions that speak to private sector ownership of capital and eschew public ownership of commercial operations to influence their choices of the method of achieving economic development. It is suggested that the private sector in small countries like Barbados is too small to raise the kind of capital to fund operations of the size that is needed to be competitive in world markets. Until such time as capital markets are developed, the government is well placed to provide such capital. It cannot be expected that such capital will be raised from international financial institutions, but resources can be obtained from the capital markets and from government's domestic revenue resources.

## A SUGGESTED APPROACH: BUILD, OPERATE AND TRANSFER

It is the author's view that the most important decisions which government can take to offset some of the challenges of globalization is to adopt a "build, operate and transfer" approach to development. The approach that is being recommended here is for government to build, operate and then transfer (BOT) the assets to the private sector. There is a tendency to consider that this BOT approach should start with the private sector's building social overhead capital and subsequently transferring it to government, but in the case of commercial operations the reverse BOT approach is highly applicable to the case of small countries. That is, government should build these enterprises, operate them and subsequently transfer them to private ownership. In this way significantly larger enterprises can be built and developed than is possible by the private sector alone. Indeed, in a world of mergers and mega mergers, the larger the operation, the more likely it is to reap the economies of scale so important for competitiveness. These operations could then be disposed of or privatized before some of the rigidities and subsequent inefficiencies sometimes associated with government ownership of commercial activities set it.

## COMPULSORY SAVINGS, PENSION FUNDS AND THEIR ROLE IN FINANCING ECONOMIC DEVELOPMENT

The second most important initiative for small centers like Barbados is to use the compulsory savings system to raise the savings rate. Compulsory savings schemes should be made an important plank of savings and should be developed into a major vehicle for promoting accelerated development, and capital market deepening. The basis for this can be the National Insurance Scheme.

The National Insurance scheme, another proactive statutory board, was established in 1966 to provide needed social benefits to the population. These included sickness, maternity, injury, severance and old age pensions. Prior to the structural adjustment exercise in 1991 the rates at which the National Insurance scheme charged income earners and self-employed persons were 9.75% and 13.75%, respectively. The maximum contribution permitted was on incomes of $31,200 and the cap on benefits was related to the cap on contributions. Levies were subsequently imposed on employers and contributions to NIS equivalent to 8.25% of emoluments of each employee (see Holder and Prescod, 1984). During the mid- to late-1980s a number of levies were introduced to supplement government revenues. These included a health levy, a transportation levy, a training levy and an unemployment benefit scheme. The assets of this Fund are tremendous and, if widely deployed, can contribute significantly to accelerated economic growth and to a repositioning of the economy for the twenty-first century while maintaining the integrity of the Fund. If measures are taken to increase the compulsory savings rate, the potential for accelerating development can be tremendous.

## IS SMALLER GOVERNMENT BETTER GOVERNMENT?

The question of an appropriate size of government has permeated the literature on public finance for many years. There is no single or simple answer. Increasingly the view tended to prevail that the size of the fiscal deficit and not the size of government was the key to stabilizing economies. This formed the basis of most of the structural adjustment policies. Direct monetary controls became unacceptable and greater reliance was placed on fiscal policy.

As the trend toward liberalization of economies widens and globalization and technological changes make it more and more difficult to isolate financial flows, central banks have had to relinquish many of the tools that once formed the arsenal of monetary management. At the same time smaller government was advocated and privatization policies and commercial provision of services were encouraged. In the future should governments become smaller, it is more likely therefore to be private sector activities which will be the source of instabilities. However, it is doubtful whether countries will now become more stable because governments are smaller.

It is most unlikely, given the need for some public goods, given the likely continued occurrence of market failure, and given the several externalities that result from government activity, that the role of government will be substantially reduced. The search must therefore be for productivity improvements in the public sector.

Typical marginal cost pricing cannot be applied to measure efficiency and productivity, where one is evaluating service value, especially where there are externalities. Normally, if price exceeds marginal cost, efficiency will be improved if output is raised, since the increment to output will be greater than the cost of producing it. However, in nonmarket situations where neither price nor cost is clear, then benchmarks need to be devised.

Also, empirical work on the relative cost of private and public enterprises in other countries is ambivalent. The work of Bocherding et al. (1982) suggests that in the case of public production, in most fields where both public and private sectors are engaged (airlines, banking, bus service, housing, hospitals) there is greater efficiency in the private enterprise. Few studies, for example, the RAND study by Ross (1988), have found that public sector enterprises were, in some cases, more efficient than the private sector. The RAND study was conducted on a disaggregated basis.

Also, there is a presumption that all government organizations are nonmarket organizations and that all private organizations are market organizations. This however, is not necessarily so. The more appropriate distinction is the "market" and "nonmarket" type operation, be it government or private, rather than to conclude that all nonmarket operations are government and that all private sector operations are market-type operations.

The challenge is also in measurement of outputs and performance. Where measurement of outputs is essentially difficult to achieve and the challenge exists of relating the cost of inputs to the "value" of outputs where this is not a monetary value, then the task of measuring performance becomes more complex, irrespective of whether the entity is government-owned or private.

An agency approach to ensuring improved productivity is also another possibility that governments might adopt. However, though agency problems are present in all organizations, they are especially acute in the government sector because oversight often is much more diffused and activities are more difficult to monitor. For these reasons direct government provision of services tends to be less efficient. However, when government-subsidized goods and services are largely private-sector in nature, customers can often monitor outcomes. Nevertheless, choice among providers leads to disciplining of private suppliers to work in the public interest, a feature that is captured in the term "transparency." These are techniques and approaches to improving the public provision of goods and services but they are not a substitute for government.

## REFORM OF THE PUBLIC SECTOR

While there may appear to be no direct link between public finance and public sector reform, to the extent that efficiencies can be achieved and operational costs reduced, public sector reform can have a substantial impact on government finances.

Improved measures of government output, an appreciation of the internalities (such as standards and goals) are therefore essential in effecting this transition. Traditional techniques such as strategic planning, information feedback mechanisms, evaluation of new policies and performances are observable transfers of these techniques to the public sector from the private sector.

It was thought by specialists in the field that performance contracts, which were on the increase internationally and which at one time were used as a means of increasing productivity and reducing costs, were the answer.

However, the results have proven to be mixed. The real effects on incentives depend on several factors, many of which go beyond the definition of the contract itself.

There is, however, common acceptance of the view that as a measure of allocating resources, markets are more efficient than governments. Wolf (1988), for example, points out that from the viewpoint of allocating resources, markets are more efficient and that allocative efficiency and dynamic efficiency (sustaining a higher rate of economic growth over time) are higher in market-oriented systems. The challenge is to accelerate the process in both the public and private sectors, and to concentrate on ensuring efficient and transparent processes in both sectors. In small developing countries where there are diseconomies of scale, underdeveloped markets and externalities such as educational exposure, technological exposure and business awareness to be gained, there is a case for government's playing an important role in improving and extending market processes. Leaving these initiatives to the private sector alone may prolong the process even in the private sector itself.

Because of the concentration on improving sectors rather than processes. Privatization is often seen as one way of promoting improved productivity and of accelerating the process of attaining efficiency and transparency. The question often arises: should privatization be an end in itself or a means to the end of achieving greater economic growth? Developing countries need to answer this question on a case-by-case basis rather than be caught in the most current philosophy. Countries generally need to differentiate the varying philosophies and focus on the facts. Aid and incentives are another such area where the philosophy differs from the facts. Almost half of the U.S. population depends, at least in part, on federal aid in one form or another. This is similarly the case in many European countries, yet International Financial Institutions frown upon incentives and subsidies in developing countries. However, they do support poverty alleviation policies in these countries.

Corporatization, a slightly modified form of commercialization, is a much discussed technique for improving efficiency. It is a hybrid form falling between government ownership and privatization that seeks to improve efficiency and reduce transfers from the public to the private sector. It is a brand of decentralization in that reallocation decisions move from the central administration to lower levels of the public sector. It has been used more successfully in Barbados, though the term was not used, in the case of government-owned enterprises, some of whom have been successful.

Other changes in organizational structure are instructive. In the United States, changes in the health care market were marked by greater competitiveness and accelerated the process of organizational changes. Hospitals moved from relatively benign to competitive environments. They appointed smaller and more risk-taking boards, focused on strategy and on increased accountability. However, there have been criticisms that the accessibility to health and other social services has suffered in the United States as missions and goals were subsumed to the emphasis on systems. This suggests the need for balance between achieving competitiveness and ensuring that the "raison d'etre" of the establishment is being met. Government organizations must therefore embrace change but must not lose sight of their mission and their goals.

Generally, however, the objectives of growth need to be weighed against other objectives of improving the standard of living. Barbados has tended to place greater emphasis on the latter, but in the process has been able to achieve creditable rates of economic growth (see the UNDP Human Development Reports, 1994 through 1999). However, in a globalized world where raw competitiveness is the yardstick for survival, there may be a need to shift priorities so that growth feeds improvement in the standard of living. Without going the route of the Asian tigers, a compromise philosophy is possible. It may well be that a standard of living has been achieved in Barbados which can now permit sustainable growth to become a greater priority.

# Selected Bibliography

Ahluawlie, M.S. 1974. "Income Inequality, Some Dimensions of the Problem," *Finance and Development*. September.

Arranovic, D. 1964. *Economic Growth and External Debt*. Baltimore: IBRD.

Arranovic, D. 1967. "The Influence of the Burden and the Problem of Flexibility," in D. Krivine, ed. *Fiscal and Monetary Problems in Developing States*. New York: Praeger.

Atkinson, A. 1999. "Is Rising Income Inequality Inevitable?" World Institute for Development Economics Research. The United Nations University, Finland. December.

Bahl, R.W. 1971. "A Regression Approach to Tax Effort and Tax Ratio Analysis." *IMF Staff Papers*, 18 November.

Baptiste, L.P. 1976. "Public Finance in Trinidad and Tobago." Paper Prepared for the Eighth Regional Program of Monetary Studies Conference. December.

Best, L. 1971. "Size and Survival," in N. Girvan and O. Jefferson, eds. *Readings in the Political Economy of the Caribbean*. Kingston: New World Group.

Bird, R.M. 1970. *Taxation and Development: Lessons from Colombian Experience*. Cambridge: Harvard University Press.

Bird, R. M. and Goldman, O. eds. 1964, revised 1975. *Readings on Taxation in Developing Countries*. Baltimore: Johns Hopkins University Press.

Boughton, J.N. and Sarwar Latee, K., eds. 1995. *Fifty Years after Bretton Woods*. Washington, DC: IMF World Bank Group.

Bocherding, T.E., Pommerehne, W.W. and Schneider, F. 1982. "Comparing Efficiency of Private and Public Production: The Evidence for Five Countries." Institute for Empirical Research in Economics, University of Zurich, Switzerland.

Bristow, John. 1993. *The Structure of a Value Added Tax*. Washington, DC: IMF.

Chand, Cheetal. 1975. "Measuring Budget Impact in Malaysia." Unpublished working paper of the IMF Staff Projects.

Chelliah, R.J. 1971. "Trends in Taxation in Developing Countries." *IMF Staff Papers* 18 July.

Chelliah, R.J., Bass, H.J. and Kelly, M.R. 1975. "Tax Ratios and Tax Effort in Developing Countries, 1969–71." *IMF Staff Papers* 22 March.

Chenery, H.B. and Taylor, L. 1969. "Development Patterns among Countries and Over Time." *Review of Economics and Statistics*. Vol. 1 No. 4 November.

Cohen, B.I. 1966. "Measuring the Short-run Impact of a Country's Import Restrictions on Its Imports." *Quarterly Journal of Economics*. August.

Craigwell, R., Dalrymple, K. and Moore, M. 1996. "Tax Reform in Barbados: The Development of a Value added Tax." Central Bank of Barbados. Working Paper. November.

Dawes, H.N. 1982. *Public Finance and Economic Development: Spotlight in Jamaica.* Washington, DC: University Press of America.

Deane, Phyllis. 1989. *The State and the Economic System: An Introduction to the History of Political Economy.* Oxford: Oxford University Press.

Demas, William. 1965. *The Economics of Development in Small Countries with Special Reference to the Caribbean.* Montreal: McGill University Press.

Dernberg, Thomas. 1975. "Fiscal Analysis in the Federal Republic of Germany: The Cyclically Neutral Budget." *IMF Staff Papers* 22 November.

Diamond, P. 1989. "Government Expenditure and Economic Growth: An Empirical Investigation." IMF Working Paper 45 May.

Diamond, P. 1995. "Government Provision and Regulation of Economic Support in Old Age." Annual World Bank Conference in Development and Economics. Washington, DC: World Bank.

Due, J.F. 1970, 1988 Revised. *Indirect Taxation in Developing Economies.* Baltimore: Johns Hopkins University Press.

Due, J.F. and Friedlaender, A.F. 1973. *Government Finance. Economics of the Public Sector.* Homewood: Richard D. Irwin.

Duncan, C.D., ed. 1989. *Public Finance and Fiscal Issues in Barbados and the OECS.* Cave Hill: University of the West Indies, Faculty of Social Sciences.

Enmeze, C. 1973. "Structure of Public Expenditure in Selected Developing Countries: A Time Study." *Manchester School of Economic and Social Studies.* Vol. XLI No. 4 December.

Feldstein, M.S. 1980. *The American Economy in Transition.* Chicago: University of Chicago Press.

Fitzgerald, E.V.K. 1993. *The Macroeconomics of Development Finance—A Kaleckian Analysis of the Semi-industrial Economy.* New York: St. Martin's Press.

Fitzgerald, Randall. 1988. *When Government Goes Private: Successful Alternatives to Public Services.* New York: Universe Books.

Forte, G. and A. Peacock, eds. 1985. *Public Expenditure and Government Growth.* Oxford: Blackwell.

Gandhi, V.P. 1971. "Wagner's Law of Public Expenditure—Do Recent Cross-section Studies Confirm It?" *Public Finance* Vol. XXVI No. 1.

Goffman, T.J. and Mahar, D.J. 1971. "The Growth of Public Expenditures in Selected Developing Nations. Six Caribbean Countries, 1950–1965." *Public Finance* Vol. XXVI No. 1.

Goode, Richard. 1967. "Impact of Fiscal Measures," in D. Krivine, ed. *Fiscal and Monetary Problems in Developing States.* New York: Praeger.

Goode, Richard. 1964. *The Individual Income Tax.* Washington, DC: Brookings Institution.

Grossman, P.J. 1988. "Government and Economic Growth: A Non-Linear Relationship." *Public Choice* Vol. 56 No. 2.

Guerard, Michele. 1975. "Fiscal versus Trade Incentives for Industrialization." *Finance and Development*, Symposium, Vol. 10.

Harris, S.E. 1947. *Keynes Influence on Theory and Public Policy: The New Economics.* New York: Alfred A. Knopf.

Hinrichs, H.H. 1965. "Determinants of Government Revenue Sharing in Less Developed Countries." *Economic Journal* Vol. LXXV No. 299 September.

Hinrichs, H. 1966. *A General Theory of Tax Structure Change During Economic Development.* Cambridge, MA: Harvard Law School, International Tax Program.

Holder, C. and Prescod, R. 1984. "Income Distribution in Barbados." Collection of Unpublished Papers, Central Bank of Barbados.

Howard, M. 1989. *Dependence and Development in Barbados, 1945–1985.* Bridgetown: Carib Research and Publications Inc.

Iyoha, M.A. 1975. "The Inflationary effect of a Government Deficit in a Developing Economy." *Social and Economic Studies* Vol. 24 No. 1 March.

Jimenez, E. 1999. "Equity, Decentralization of Social Services, ABCD-LAC." Paper Presented for the Annual World Bank Conference on Development in Latin America and the Caribbean. Chile. June.

Jolly, R. 1999. "Global Inequality." World Institute for Development Economics Research. The United Nations University, Finland. December.

Kadar, B. 1970. "Small Countries in the World Economy." *Studies on Developing Countries* No. 34. Budapest: Center for Afro-Asian Research of the Hungarian Academy of Social Science.

Kennedy, C. 1966. "Keynesian Theory in an Open Economy." *Social and Economic Studies* Vol. 15 No. 1 March.

Keynes, J.M. 1936. *The General Theory of Employment Interest and Money.* New York: Harcourt Brace and World.

Krause-Junk G., ed. 1989. "Public Finance and Steady State Economic Growth." Proceedings of the 45th Congress of the International Institute of Public Finance, Buenos Aires.

Lall, S. 1969. "A Note on Public Expenditure in Developing Countries." *Economic Journal* Vol. LXXIX No. 314 June.

Landau, D.L. 1986. "Government and Economic Growth in Less Developed Countries: An Empirical Study for 1960–1980." *Economic Development and Cultural Change* Vol. 35 No. 1 October.

Levin, J. 1970. "Management of Debt in Developing Countries." *Finance and Development Quarterly* No. 2 June.

Lewis, S.R. 1984. *Taxation for Development: Principles of Accounting.* Oxford: Oxford University Press.

Lewis, W.A. 1969. *The Principles of Economic Planning.* London: Allen & Unwin.

Lotz, J. F. and Morss, E.R. 1967. "Measuring Tax Effort in Developing Countries." *IMF Staff Papers* 14 November.

Mansfield, C.Y. 1972. "Elasticity and Buoyancy of a Tax System: A Method Applied to Paraguay." *IMF Staff Papers* July.

Marsden, Keith. 1983. "Links between Taxes and Economic Growth: Some Empirical Evidence." World Bank Staff Working Paper 605, Washington, DC.

Martin, A. and Lewis, W.A. 1956. "Patterns of Public Expenditure." *Manchester School of Economic and Social Studies.* September.

Mascoll, C. and Harding, N. 1992. "The Effects of Changing C.E.T Rates." The Central Bank of Barbados (mimeo) September.

Mukherji, J. 2000. "Barbados and Hong Kong: A Tale of Two Islands." *Credit Week.* Standard and Poors. April.

Musgrave, R.A. 1959. *The Theory of Public Finance.* New York: McGraw-Hill.

Musgrave, R.A. and Musgrave, P.B. 1984. *Public Finance in Theory and Practice.* New York: McGraw-Hill.

Newbery, D.G.M and Stern, N.H., eds. 1987. *The Theory of Taxation for Developing Countries.* Oxford: Oxford University Press for the World Bank.

Nunberg, Barbara. 1999. "Public Sector Pay and Employment Reform—A Review of World Bank Experience." World Bank Discussion Papers No. 68, Washington, DC.

Odle, M. 1976. "The Evolution of Public Expenditure: The Case of a Structurally Dependent Economy." Mona, Jamaica. Institute of Social and Economic Research.

Olson, Mancur. 1982. *The Rise and Decline of Nations.* New Haven: Yale University Press.

Osborne, David and Gaebler, Ted. 1992. *Reinventing Government: How the Entrepreneurial Spirit Is Transforming the Public Sector.* Reading, MA: Addison-Wesley.

Peterson, H. 1981. "Tax Systems and Economic Growth," in Herbert Gierson, ed. *Toward an Explanation of Economic Growth*. Symposium 1980. Institute fur Weltwirtschaft an der Universistat Idiel.

Pleskovic, B. and Stiglitz, S.J., eds. 1997. *Annual World Bank Conference on Development Economics*. Washington, DC: World Bank.

Prest, A.R. 1969. "Compulsory Lending Schemes." *IMF Staff Papers* 26 March.

Prest, A.R. 1962. *Public Finance in Underdeveloped Countries*. London: Weidenfeld and Nicholson.

Prest, A.R. 1957. *Fiscal Survey of the British Caribbean*. London: Her Majesty's Stationary Office.

Robinson, E.A.G. 1963. "The Size of the Nation and the Cost of Administration," in E.A.G. Robinson, ed. *Economic Consequence of the Size of Nations*. New York: St. Martin's Press.

Roe, A.R. 1968. "The Government Revenue Share in Poorer African Countries." *Economic Journal* Vol. XXVIII No. 310 June.

Rosen, S. and Weinberg, B. 1997. "Incentives, Efficiency and Government Provision of Public Services" in *Annual World Bank Conference on Development Economics,* ed. B. Plesovic and J. Stiglitz. Washington, DC: World Bank.

Ross, R.L. 1984. *Choosing Roles and Missions for Government and the Private Sector: A Preliminary Framework and Analysis*. RAND November.

Ross, R.L. 1988. *Government and the Private Sector: Who Should Do What?* New York: Taylor & Francis.

Rubinson, R. 1977. "Dependence, Government Revenues and Economic Growth 1955–1970." *Studies in Comparative International Development* Vol. 12 No. 2.

Rupprecht, E.O. 1974. "How Big Is Government?" *Finance and Development* Vol. 11 No. 1 March.

Samuelson, P. 1958a. "Aspects of Public Expenditure Theories." *Review of Economics and Statistics* Vol. 40.

Samuelson, P. 1958b. "The Pure Theory of Public Expenditures," *Review of Economics and Statistics* Vol. 40.

Seers, D. 1962. "The Limitations of the Special Case." *Bulletin of the Oxford Institute of Economics and Statistics*. May.

Smith, P. 1993. "Measuring Human Development." *Asian Economic Journal* Vol. 7 No. 11.

Smith, P. and Ulph, A.M. 1995. "A Comparative Study of Flexibility in the Response of National Economies to the Oil-Price Shocks," in Tony Killick, ed. *The Flexible Economy*. London: Routledge.

Smith P. and Wahba, J. 1997. "The Role of Public Finance in Economic Development: An Empirical Investigation," *Discussion Papers in Economics and Econometrics* No. 9427. University of Southampton.

Tanzi, V., Newbery, D.M.G. and Stern, N., eds. 1987. *Modern Tax Theory for Development Countries*. Baltimore: IBRD.

Thorn, R.S. 1967. "The Evolution of Public Finance During Economic Development." *Manchester School of Economic and Social Studies*. January.

Thurow, L.C. 1975. "The Economics of Public Finance." *National Tax Journal* 28 June.

Tun Wai, and Partick, H. 1973. "Stock and Bond Issues and Capital Markets in Less Developed Countries." *IMF Staff Papers* 20 July.

United Nations Development Program. 1994. *UNDP Human Development Report*. New York: Oxford University Press.

Wagner, A. 1958. "Three Extracts on Public Finance." in Richard A. Musgrave and Alan Peacock, eds. *Classics in the Theory of Public Finance*. London: Macmillan.

Wijnbergen, Van Sweder. 1989. "External Debt, Inflation and the Public Sector: Toward Fiscal Policy for Sustainable growth." *World Bank Economic Review* Vol. 3 No. 3 September.

Williams, M. 1991a. "Tax Effort, Tax Capacity and Tax Elasticity—A Review of Barbados' Tax Performance in the 1980s." Barbados Economic Society Seminar on Fiscal Reform. May.

Williams, M. 1991b. "Tax Reform in Barbados in the 1980s." Bridgetown: Central Bank of Barbados, mimeo.

Williams, M. 1977. "The Structure and Performance of the Government Sector: Barbados 1950–1976." Msc. Thesis. Cave Hill: University of the West Indies.

Williams, M. 1976. "The Conflict between Growth, Stabilization and Development Roles of Fiscal Policy in Barbados, 1964–1976." Paper presented at the Eighth Regional Program of Monetary Studies Conference. December.

Wolf, C. Jr. 1993. *Markets or Governments: Choosing between Imperfect Alternatives*. 2nd edition. Cambridge, MA: MIT Press.

Wolf, C. Jr. 1988. *Markets or Governments*. Cambridge, MA: MIT Press.

Wulf, Luc de. 1975. "Fiscal Incidence Studies in Developing Countries: Survey and Critique." *IMF Staff Papers* 22 March.

# Index

**About the Author**

MARION V. WILLIAMS is Governor of the Central Bank of Barbados, where she previously served as economist, adviser, and Deputy Governor. Her research over the past three decades has focused on the special circumstances of developing countries, with particular reference to the Caribbean. She is author of the book *Liberating a Regulated Banking System: The Caribbean Case.*